Robert T. Lattey

A Handy Book

on the practice and procedure before the Judicial Committee of Her Majesty's Most

Honourable Privy Council

Robert T. Lattey

A Handy Book
on the practice and procedure before the Judicial Committee of Her Majesty's Most Honourable Privy Council

ISBN/EAN: 9783337194895

Printed in Europe, USA, Canada, Australia, Japan

Cover: Foto ©Suzi / pixelio.de

More available books at **www.hansebooks.com**

VALUABLE LAW WORKS

PUBLISHED BY

STEVENS AND SONS,
LIMITED,
119 & 120, CHANCERY LANE, LONDON, W.C.

JANUARY, 1891.

The Annual Practice for 1890-91.—Edited by THOMAS SNOW, Barrister-at-Law; CHARLES BURNEY, a Chief Clerk of the Hon. Mr. Justice Chitty, Editor of "Daniell's Chancery Forms"; and F. A. STRINGER, of the Central Office, Author of "Oaths and Affirmations." 2 Vols. Demy 8vo. Price 21s. cloth.

"A book which every practising English lawyer must have."—*Law Quarterly Review.*

Greenwood's Practice of Conveyancing, with Concise Precedents.—A Manual of the Practice of Conveyancing. Showing the present Practice relating to the daily routine of Conveyancing in Solicitors' Offices, to which are added Concise Common Forms and Precedents in Conveyancing. Eighth Edition. By HARRY GREENWOOD, M.A., LL.D., Barrister-at-Law. Demy 8vo. 1891. Price 16s. cloth.

"One of those books which no lawyer's bookshelf should be without. .... A complete guide to Conveyancing."—*Law Gazette,* Dec. 4, 1890.

Smith's Compendium of Mercantile Law.—Tenth Edition. By JOHN MACDONELL, Esq., one of the Masters of the Supreme Court, assisted by GEO. HUMPHREYS, Esq., Barrister-at-Law. 2 Vols. Royal 8vo. 1890. Price 2l. 2s. cloth.

"Of the greatest value to the mercantile lawyer."—*Law Times.*

Roscoe's Digest of the Law of Evidence in Criminal Cases.—Eleventh Edition. By HORACE SMITH and GILBERT GEORGE KENNEDY, Esqrs., Metropolitan Police Magistrates. Demy 8vo. 1890. Price 1l. 11s. 6d. cloth.

Roscoe's Digest of the Law of Evidence on the Trial of Actions at Nisi Prius.—Fifteenth Edition. By MAURICE POWELL, Esq., Barrister-at-Law. 2 Vols. Demy 8vo 1891. (*Nearly ready.*)

Prideaux's Precedents in Conveyancing.—With Dissertations on its Law and Practice. Fourteenth Edition. By FREDERICK PRIDEAUX, late Professor of the Law of Real and Personal Property to the Inns of Court, and JOHN WHITCOMBE, Esqrs., Barristers-at-Law. 2 Vols. Royal 8vo. 1889. Price 3l. 10s. cloth.

"The most useful work out on Conveyancing."—*Law Journal.*

Pollock's Digest of the Law of Partnership.—Incorporating the Partnership Act, 1890. Fifth Edition. By SIR FREDERICK POLLOCK, Bart., Barrister-at-Law. Author of "Principles of Contract," "The Law of Torts," &c. Demy 8vo. 1890. Price 8s. 6d. cloth.

Pollock's Law of Torts.—A Treatise on the Principles of Obligations arising from Civil Wrongs in the Common Law. Second Edition, to which is added the draft of a Code of Civil Wrongs prepared for the Government of India. By Sir FREDERICK POLLOCK, Bart., Barrister-at-Law. Demy 8vo. 1890. Price 1l. 1s. cloth.

Pollock's Principles of Contract.—Being a Treatise on the General Principles relating to the Validity of Agreements in the Law of England. Fifth Edition. With a New Chapter. By Sir FREDERICK POLLOCK, Bart., Barrister-at-Law. Demy 8vo. 1889. Price 1l. 8s. cloth.

₊ *A Catalogue of Law Works*

Pitt-Lewis' Complete Practice of the County Courts, including that in Admiralty and Bankruptcy, embodying the County Courts Act, 1888, and other existing Acts, Rules, Forms, and Costs, wi h full Alphabetical Index to Official Forms, Additional Forms, and General Index. Fourth Edition. By G. PITT-LEWIS, Esq., Q.C., M.P., Recorder of Poole. 2 Vols. Demy 8vo. 1890. Price 2l. 10s. cloth.

. The Volumes sold separately, price, each, 30s.

"**The Standard County Court Practice.**"—*Solicitors' Journal.*

Godefroi's Law of Trusts and Trustees.—Second Edition. By HENRY GODEFROI, Esq., Barrister-at-Law. Royal 8vo. 1891. (*Nearly ready.*)

Goddard's Treatise on the Law of Easements.—Fourth Edition. By JOHN LEYBOURN GODDARD, Esq., Barrister-at-Law. Demy 8vo. 1891. (*Nearly ready.*)

Palmer's Company Precedents.—Conveyancing and other Forms and Precedents for use in relation to Companies subject to the Companies Acts, 1862 to 1890. Arranged as follows:—Promoters, Prospectuses, Agreements, Memoranda and Articles of Association, Resolutions, Notices, Certificates, Private Companies, Power of Attorney, Debentures and Debenture Stock, Policies, Petitions, Writs, Statements of Claim, Judgments and Orders, Reconstruction, Amalgamation, Arrangements, Special Acts, Provisional Orders, Winding-up. With Copious Notes and an Appendix containing the Acts and Rules. Fifth Edition. By FRANCIS BEAUFORT PALMER, assisted by CHARLES MACNAGHTEN, Esqrs., Barristers-at-Law. Royal 8vo. 1891. (*Nearly ready.*)

"**In company** drafting it stands unrivalled."—*Law Times.*

Thring's Joint Stock Companies' Law.—The Law and Practice of Joint Stock and other Companies, including the Companies Acts, 1862 to 1886, with Notes, Orders, and Rules in Chancery, a Collection of Precedents of Memoranda and Articles of Association, and other Forms required in Making and Administering a Company. By Lord THRING, K.C.B., formerly the Parliamentary Counsel. Fifth Edition. By J. M. RENDEL, Esq., Barrister-at-Law. Royal 8vo. 1889. Price 1l. 10s. cloth.

"**The highest authority on the subject.**"—*The Times.*

Brooke's Notary.—A Treatise on the Office and Practice of a Notary of England. With a Full Collection of Precedents. Fifth Edition. By GEORGE F. CHAMBERS, Esq., Barrister-at-Law. Demy 8vo. 1890. Price 1l. 1s. cloth.

Edmunds' Law and Practice of Letters Patent for Inventions with the Patents Acts and Rules Annotated, and the International Convention, a full Collection of Statutes, Forms and Precedents, and an Outline of Foreign and Colonial Patent Laws, &c. By LEWIS EDMUNDS, assisted by A. WOOD RENTON, Esqrs., Barristers-at-Law. Royal 8vo. 1890. Price 1l. 12s. cloth.

Sebastian's Law of Trade Marks and their Registration, and Matters connected therewith, including a Chapter on Goodwill. Together with the Patents, Designs, and Trade Marks Acts, 1883—1888, and the Trade Marks Rules and Instructions thereunder, Forms and Precedents; the Merchandise Marks Act, 1887, and other Statutory Enactments; and the United States Statutes, 1870 to 1881, and the Rules and Forms thereunder, and the Treaty with the United States, 1877. Third Edition. By LEWIS BOYD SEBASTIAN, B.C.L., M.A., of Lincoln's Inn, Esq., Barrister-at-Law. Demy 8vo. 1890. Price 1l. 5s. cloth.

A HANDY BOOK

ON THE

PRACTICE AND PROCEDURE

BEFORE THE

JUDICIAL COMMITTEE OF HER MAJESTY'S
MOST HONOURABLE PRIVY COUNCIL.

BY

ROBERT THOMAS LATTEY,

ATTORNEY OF THE COURT OF QUEEN'S BENCH, AND OF THE HIGH COURT
OF BENGAL;
AND ADVOCATE OF THE COURTS OF BRITISH BURMAH.

LONDON:
STEVENS AND SONS,
Law Booksellers and Publishers,
119, CHANCERY LANE, FLEET STREET.
1869.

LONDON :
BRADBURY, EVANS, AND CO., PRINTERS, WHITEFRIARS

PREFACE.

ONE of the chief objects of the writer in compiling this handbook is to afford a guide to professional gentlemen practising in the superior Courts throughout India, from which an appeal is allowed to the Privy Council, in cases in which they have to send appeals to England; but at the same time the writer wishes to point out, that as the procedure is the same in all cases, whether the appeal be from India or from any other of Her Majesty's colonies or dominions, this book will be of equal assistance to those practising in any colony or dependency other than India, from which an appeal lies to the Privy Council.

Another object the writer has in view, is to make this book a strictly practical one. All references to decided cases have been purposely omitted, as the writer considers such references to be wholly unnecessary in a book such as the present. Should a necessity at any time exist to refer to decided cases, the same will be found in "Moore's Privy Council Cases," or in his "East India Appeal Cases," the index to which is so carefully arranged that an immediate reference can at once be had to the question at issue.

It is not intended in this handbook to go at any length into the various questions that would have to be discussed in what ought more properly to be termed a text-book. A treatise on the various jurisdictions of a Judicial Committee, their origin and application, would of necessity be a most voluminous work, the practical benefit of which may be doubted, the facts in each case of necessity differing.

The writer has endeavoured to point out in a concise manner the procedure in an appeal, and he has in each case given a form that may be used in the various steps of the appeal, with the intention of making the book equally useful to solicitors and agents in England having the conduct or defence of appeals pending in the Privy Council.

From practical experience in more than one colonial Court, the writer is aware that a great want of knowledge exists respecting an appeal to the Privy Council, the mode of its institution, its probable duration, and lastly, the most important item of all, the costs that an appeal will entail; upon these points especially the writer purposes directing his remarks.

ROBERT THOMAS LATTEY.

80, GRESHAM HOUSE,
OLD BROAD STREET, LONDON.

March, 1869.

INTRODUCTION.

PREVIOUS to the issuing of the Order in Council
of the 13th of June, 1853, which will be found at
page 174, there was considerable confusion as to
the procedure of a Judicial Committee. This
occasioned the Lords of the Committee to report
upon this matter, the result being the issuing of
the said Order of the 13th June, 1853.

Shortly after the issuing of this Order, Her
Majesty was pleased to issue the further Order
of the 31st March, 1855 (*vide* page 154), giving
the Judicial Committee power to make any order
or direction which, in their opinion, the justice of
any particular case might require.

No printed orders have been issued under this
authority, but what may be termed a settled
practice is now established. In the following

pages will be found a *resumé* of this practice, but, at the same time, the reader must bear in mind that a Judicial Committee is a Court having unlimited powers, and can hardly be said to be bound by any practice at all—certainly not in the sense in which this expression would be used when referring to any ordinary Court.

There is not any express rule binding practitioners to any particular form. All that is required is that the forms used should sufficiently state the facts that will support the order asked for. Care must be taken that all petitions that have to be referred to the Committee are addressed to Her Majesty in Council, and that all other petitions for *ad interim* orders are addressed to the Judicial Committee.

In the following pages will be found a concise set of ordinary forms that may be used, and that it is believed will be sufficient in every case; but the practitioner must remember such forms are not issued under any authority.

CONTENTS.

———◆———

PRACTICAL INFORMATION

RESPECTING

FORWARDING AN APPEAL,

AND

REMITTANCE OF NECESSARY FUNDS.

BEFORE appealing to the Privy Council, the appellant should be careful that he has exhausted every right of appeal open to him in the courts of the country from which the appeal is made; any omission in this respect will be fatal to his application, as the Privy Council will only entertain appeals from courts of last instance.

The appellant should be equally careful, previous to appealing to the Privy Council, to apply to the court appealed from for liberty to appeal; he should do so even in cases in which such court has apparently no power to grant the application. It is sometimes a question of great nicety whether such power exists or not; and as this application cannot injure the appellant's position, and may in certain cases considerably benefit him when before the Privy Council, the advisability in all cases of making it is obvious.

The appellant having satisfied himself on this point, next proceeds to appoint his agent in England; this he usually does by directing a power of attorney to such person in manner hereafter pointed out at page 13 (*et sequitur*). It is then necessary for him to determine whether he will cause the record to be printed abroad, or whether he will have it printed in England; each of these courses is at present (*a*) open to him. Should he decide upon having it printed abroad, he should at once forward the power of attorney to his agent, with instructions to retain counsel. Should the appellant wish to leave the appointment of counsel to his agent, he ought to send short instructions as to the nature of the case, so that the agent may be properly guided in his selection.

The respondent should also follow a similar

(*a*) Owing to the careless manner in which some printed records have been forwarded to the Privy Council, it is questionable whether a rule will not shortly be passed directing all printing to be done in England.

course so soon as he knows the case will be appealed.

One great objection to the record being printed abroad is, that a successful appellant is unable to recover the cost of printing from the respondent, whilst if the record is printed in England such charges are always included in the solicitor's bill, and are allowed on taxation.

The cost of appearing and retaining counsel for appellant or respondent, and letter to colonial agent, is 8*l*. 10*s*.

If the appellant prefers the record being printed in England, he should remit sufficient money to his agent for payment of a certified copy of it, and also for perusing the papers. The amount required for this purpose entirely depends upon the number of folios in the record.

The fee allowed for perusing is at the rate of 6*s*. 8*d*. for each three brief sheets, containing together fifteen folios; the cost of the certified copy is at the rate of 1*s*. per brief sheet of stationers' copying, so that in a case in which the record contains, say 1000 folios (seventy-two words constituting a folio), the cost for perusing would be 22*l*. 6*s*. 8*d*., and the copy would come to not less than

10*l.* A record which only contains 1000 folios is comparatively a small one. One thousand folios would occupy about sixty-seven pages (taking fifteen folios as the average contents of each page), or seventeen folio sheets (each folio sheet containing four printed pages). The cost of printing in England averages from 35*s.* to 2*l.* per printed folio sheet; this sum includes the cost of printing off 100 copies, therefore the cost of printing 1000 folios may be taken in round figures at 30*l.* The agent is allowed two guineas per diem for examining the copy transcript with the original. This examination has to be very carefully conducted, and it is considered a fair average to examine twenty-four printed pages per day; accordingly the cost of this examination for 1000 folios may be taken at 6*l.* 5*s.*, or three days' attendance; the cost for correcting such proofs will be 17*l.* 17*s* (*a*).

The total sum that must be sent to the appellant's agent for perusing, printing, and examining a record of 1000 folios, including other small items, may be taken to be 90*l.* to 100*l.*

The appellant's agent would also require

(*a*) This sum is allowed to the agents on each side.

a sum of (say) 10*l.* for the preparation of the petition of appeal.

The sum which the respondent's agent would require for perusing papers and examining, and correcting proofs, would be 50*l.* to 60*l.*

When the record is printed abroad, the appellant's agent is allowed for perusing at the rate of one guinea for each printed folio sheet, irrespective of the number of the folios it actually contains ; and as the average number of folios in a folio sheet is forty, instead of sixty as in England, each agent would require for each 1000 folios, say 27*l.*, to be remitted for this perusal.

The colonial correspondent should also inform his agent if he wishes the printed case to be settled by two counsel ; and in heavy matters it is certainly most advisable it should be so settled.

It is very difficult to give any general estimate of the cost of settling a case; the following may, however, be of use :—

When the record contains, say 1000 folios, counsel's fees for settling case would be from fifteen to twenty guineas each, and a consultation fee of five guineas each. A fair average number of folios for a case may be taken from fifty to eighty; the incidental costs, including the printing, may be taken at 20*l.*; so that the total amount each agent would want would be about 75*l.*

The number of folios in the record is not in all cases a guide as to the amount of counsel's fees. In appeals in which the record is short, and the whole case depends upon strictly foreign law, a larger fee than one calculated on the actual number of folios in the record is necessary.

During the progress of the appeal, *ad interim* orders are generally necessary on each side; a sum of 10*l.* may be included for these charges.

The hearing fees are generally estimated with reference to the number of folios in the record, and are usually half as much again as those marked for settlement of case, and vary from, say twenty-five to 150 guineas to the senior counsel, and twenty to 100 to the junior one, with a consultation fee of five guineas each.

In a record of 1000 folios, the hearing fee for the leader may be taken at forty guineas, the fee to the junior at thirty guineas, with a consultation fee of five guineas to each. The argument may be considered to occupy two days, so that each counsel would require a refresher of ten guineas, and a further fee of five guineas each, to attend and hear judgment, making a total of, say 121*l.*; the other incidental expenses may be taken at 30*l.*; and as the appellant's and respondent's costs are the same, the agents on each side would require a sum of, say 150*l.*

The costs of the final order, and other expenses attending it, may be taken at 30*l.* on each side.

It can, from these figures, be roughly estimated that an appeal printed in England, the record of which contains 1000 folios, and is before the Judicial Committee for three days, will cost the appellant 360*l.* and the respondent 320*l.*; and if the record is printed abroad, the cost on either side will be about 300*l.*

The cost of applying to the Judicial Committee for special leave to appeal, in a great measure depends on the length of the documents that have to be perused; in ordinary cases, this amount may be estimated from 40*l.* to 50*l.*

It is often advisable, before taking any active steps in an appeal, to get an opinion of counsel as to the advisability of appealing;

the costs for such an opinion will entirely depend on the question at issue, and also whether the case is submitted to one or two counsel; the cost of such an opinion when the point at issue turns upon pure questions of foreign law is much greater than one which is taken on a question regulated by English principles. The sum of 50*l*. may be taken in round figures to be a fair average for an opinion settled in conference between two counsel.

It is often advisable, previous to appealing to the Privy Council, to be satisfied respecting the rules or regulations then in force regulating appeals from the court appealed from, and for this purpose to refer to the English agent to get a copy of such rules or regulations from the Council office; the costs of this will depend on the length of the document to be copied, the charge for copying being at the rate of 5*s*. per brief sheet, and a search fee of 10*s*. The sum of 5*l*. may be taken to be a fair average amount for this purpose.

At page 110, *et sequitur*, will be found some precedents of bills of costs, a perusal of which will enable colonial agents better to understand the manner in which the charges in an appeal are made out. In considering these bills, it must be remembered that they are only made out as between party and party, and so only contain the actual strict charges that are usually allowed; on taxation, all correspondence with colonial agents, &c., is omitted, these charges not being allowed on a party and party taxation.

In all courts in England the principle of only allowing, as against the defeated party, those costs which were absolutely necessary for the conduct of the litigation, is adopted; but the right of the solicitor to charge his client with all other reasonable charges which he has incurred at his client's direction, or which he was at the time the same were incurred justified as against his own client in incurring, will be allowed him; and it may be taken to be a rule that in every appeal the English solicitor will have to make some charges against his own client, whatever the result of the appeal may be.

JURISDICTION OF PRIVY COUNCIL.

THE jurisdiction of the Privy Council, or, more properly speaking, of the Judicial

Committee of the Privy Council, is divided
into two heads, the one referring to that
class of cases in which an appeal can be
brought as a matter of right, and the other
to that class of cases in which it is necessary
to obtain special leave to appeal. It may
be taken as a principle that the Crown has
an absolute inherent right in all cases to
admit of an appeal from any of its subjects
complaining of any judicial act that has
occurred out of Great Britain; but it must
be remembered, when considering this principle, that the Crown may, by an Act of
Parliament, have abrogated this right, in
which case the Privy Council is precluded
both from considering the question and from
recommending Her Majesty to do so. In
considering whether an appeal lies to Her
Majesty in Council, the first point of inquiry
is whether a right of appeal is given by any
local act or regulation; failing it being given,
the next inquiry is whether such inherent
right of the Crown is taken away. Should
it be found that a right of appeal is not
expressly taken away, it may then be concluded that a right in the Crown to admit
of an appeal does exist.

All cases in appeal, whether of right or

by special leave, must be commenced by a petition ; this petition is addressed to Her Majesty in Council, and is, in fact, the first formal step in the prosecution of the appeal after the arrival of the record.

After the petition is printed, it is referred to a Judicial Committee for a report, and the admission or non-admission of the appeal will be determined by this report.

It seems hardly necessary to point out the benefit of such a court as a Judicial Committee of the Privy Council, consisting, as it does in all cases, of the highest and most able of our English judges, who are in most cases especially associated together with reference to their peculiar knowledge of the subject matter of the appeal. There has of late years been a considerable increase in the number of appeals, and this number would, doubtless, be much added to if Her Majesty's colonial subjects were more conversant with the benefit to be derived from appealing. It only requires a slight knowledge of the simple and excellent procedure of this court to be fully convinced how perfect its system is, in enabling a correct and just judgment to be formed on the matters in dispute.

SITTINGS OF JUDICIAL COMMITTEE.

THE Judicial Committee hold three sittings in the year. These sittings are generally held in February, June, and November; and each sitting usually lasts about six weeks.

PERSONS WHO CAN APPEAR BEFORE AND ACT AS AGENTS IN THE PRIVY COUNCIL.

ALL English barristers have a right of audience before the Judicial Committee; the Committee also grant leave to any advocate of a colonial court to appear and argue before it, provided such advocate is not a practising English solicitor; but in all cases only two advocates on each side are heard, though this rule is sometimes departed from in cases in which there are various respondents who have separate interests.

All English solicitors who take out licences are, without the necessity of signing any further roll, admitted to act as agents for an appellant or respondent in the Privy

Council. Persons who are acquainted with the practice of the colonial courts are also, on application, admitted to act as agents for appellants and respondents in the matter of appeals from the colonies or dependencies in which they have been practising.

APPOINTMENT OF AGENTS IN ENGLAND.

It is always as well, when forwarding an appeal to England, or when sending instructions to England to appear for the appellant or respondent, to send a power of attorney, directed to some person, empowering him to act for the appellant or respondent, as the case may be. It need not of necessity be directed to a legal agent ; in fact, when such legal agent is a solicitor on the English roll, it is very doubtful if a power is requisite at all. The benefit, however, of sending a power is to settle any question that may arise as to the authority of the person claiming to act as the legal agent. The following are two skeleton forms of powers—one to be executed by an appellant, and the other by a respondent.

The powers must be stamped in accordance with the law of the country in which they are executed.

These powers are never lodged at the Council Office, nor are they, in fact, produced unless their production is required.

POWER FROM APPELLANTS.

KNOW ALL MEN BY THESE PRESENTS, that

State name of all appellants in full, giving addresses.

we, —————

of —————

and —————

of —————

do, and each of us doth make, ordain, con-

Name and address of person to whom power is directed.

stitute, and appoint —————

to be our true and lawful attorney, for us and in our name or names, as our attorney, to appear, and our persons to represent, in a certain appeal now depending in Her Majesty's most honourable Privy Council in

Name of court and date of decree and number of appeal.

England, from a decree of ——, bearing date the —— day of ——, and being regular appeal (a) No. ——, of ——, in which we the

The same names as above; if any others are appel-

above-named —————

are appellants, and —————

are respondents, and for us, and each of us,

(a) It is only in Indian appeals that a number is given.

and in our name or names, or in his own name as aforesaid, to enter an appearance before her most gracious Majesty in her most honourable Privy Council, or before any judicial committee thereof, and for us and in our name or names, or in the name of our counsel, to prepare, and afterwards to lodge, a case, and if necessary to make or subscribe to any statement contained in such case, or the matters and things therein appearing; and also to make any application to her Majesty in Council, or to the said judicial committee, respecting the said appeal as to our said attorney may seem expedient, or as he may be advised; and to appoint any barrister or barristers, attorney or attorneys, solicitor or solicitors, agent, or other person under him; and generally for us, and in our name or names, or in his own name as aforesaid, to do all such acts, deeds, matters, and things in the premises as fully and effectually as we could do if personally present and doing the same: we hereby ratifying and confirming, and agreeing to ratify and confirm, all and whatsoever our said attorney may do, or lawfully cause to be done, in the premises by virtue hereof. In witness whereof we have here-

lants who do not join in power, state this fact, giving names of such persons.

unto subscribed our hands and set our seals
this —— day of ——, 18—.

Signed, sealed and deli-⎫
vered by the above-named ⎮
——, at ——, in the pre- ⎬   ⊙ (Seal.) (b)
sence of —— (a). ⎭

Seal.

POWER FROM RESPONDENTS.

KNOW ALL MEN BY THESE PRESENTS, that

State names
of the re-
spondents
in full,
giving ad-
dress.

we, ————————————
of ————————————
and ————————————
of ————————————

do, and each of us doth hereby make, ordain,

Name and
address of
persons to
whom
power is to
be directed.

constitute, and appoint ————————

to be our true and lawful attorney, for us
and in our name or names, or in his own
name, as our attorney to appear to, and our
persons to represent in, a certain appeal now
depending in Her Majesty's most honourable

Name of
court, date
of decree,
and number
of appeal.
State in full.

Privy Council in England, from a decree
of ——, bearing date the —— day of ——,
and being regular appeal No. —— of 186—,

(a) It is advisable to have a fresh attestation clause
for each person.

(b) When the signature is in a foreign character, or is
by the pen of an agent, it is advisable to write under the
foreign character the English translation.

in which ——————————————————

are appellants, and we, the above-named

——————————————————

are respondents, and for us and in our name or names, or in his own name as aforesaid, to enter an appearance before her most gracious Majesty in her most honourable Privy Council, or before any judicial committee thereof, and for us and in our name or names, or in the name of our counsel, to prepare, and afterwards to lodge, a case, and if necessary to make or subscribe to any statement contained in such case, or the matters and things therein appearing; and also to make any application to Her Majesty in Council, or to the said judicial committee, respecting the said appeal or the defence thereto, as to our said attorney may seem expedient, or as he may be advised : and to appoint any barrister or barristers, attorney or attorneys, solicitor or solicitors, agent, or other person under him ; and generally for us, and in our name or names, or in his own name as aforesaid, to do all acts, deeds, matters, and things in the premises as fully and effectually as we could do if personally present and doing the same : we hereby ratifying and confirming, and agreeing to

[side note:] The same names as above: if any others are respondents who do not join in power, state this fact, giving names of such persons.

ratify and confirm, all and whatsoever our said attorney may do, or lawfully cause to be done, in the premises by virtue hereof. In witness whereof we have hereunto subscribed our hands and set our seals this —— day of ——, 18—.

Signed, sealed, and delivered by the above-named ——, at ——, in the presence of —— (a).   (Seal.) (b)

(Seal.)

CHANGE OF SOLICITOR OR AGENT DURING CONDUCT OF APPEAL.

IT is open to an appellant or respondent at any time during the progress of the appeal to change his solicitor or agent.

The mode in which this change takes place, when the former agent will consent, is by a notice in the form of a letter to the Registrar.

(a) It is advisable to have a fresh attestation clause for each person.

(b) When the signature is in a foreign character, or is by the pen of an agent, it is advisable to write under the foreign character the English translation.

The following form can be used :—

To

The Registrar of the Judicial Committee of Her Majesty's Most Honourable Privy Council.

(*Address*). Solicitor's address.

(*Date*).

BETWEEN Full title.

Appellant,

and

Respondent.

Appeal No. ——, of 18—.

SIR,

I beg to notify that I have been appointed as the (solicitor or agent) for the above-named ——, to (conduct or defend) this appeal, in the place of Mr. ——; and I shall be obliged by your notifying my appearance herein; and I hereby undertake to pay all fees which now are or hereafter may become payable in respect of this appeal.

Yours obediently,

—— (Solicitor or agent)

(For appellant or respondent).

————

(*Address*). Solicitor's address.

I, the undersigned, at present appearing as the (solicitor or agent) for the above-named (appellant or respondent), consent to the above-named Mr. —— being entered as the (solicitor or agent) on

behalf of the above-named (appellant or respondent),
in my place and stead.

      Yours obediently,

         —— (Solicitor or agent)

         (For appellant or respondent).

If the solicitor or agent refuses to give this
consent, the matter should be brought before
the Registrar ; the Registrar will either dis-
pose of the matter himself, or will refer it to
the Lords of the Judicial Committee at their
next sitting.

PRELIMINARY PROCEEDINGS IN ENGLAND.

THE first step in the Privy Council office
in an appeal in which the appellant has a
right of appeal, is the receipt at the offices
in England either of two certified printed
copies of the record, or of a certified
written copy of it. These printed or written
copies of the record must be forwarded by
the proper officer of the court from which
the appeal is made, to the Registrar of the
Judicial Committee of the Privy Council, as
provided by the Order in Council of the 13th
June, 1853. (*Vide* page 147.) Any docu-

ment not so forwarded will be refused at the Council office.

In cases in which special leave has to be obtained, it is sufficient if any ordinary copy of the record is forwarded to the appellant's solicitor or agent, as this copy will be received at the Council office provided it be accompanied by an affidavit of the agent who has received the same, setting forth the circumstances under which he received it; but it is better that such copy record, or at any rate such portions as are essential to the application, be issued under the seal of the court which has the original record. It can then be deposited in the Council office without affidavit, and will be brought before the committee by the Registrar at the hearing of the petition.

In cases in which the record has been printed abroad, it is usual for the proper officer of the colonial court to forward with the certified printed copies fifty additional copies, but this rule is not adopted in all cases, as the additional copies are sometimes forwarded direct to the agent, who in his turn deposits them at the Council office.

A proper notice of appearance having been given at the Privy Council office, the

Registrar will direct a notice to the respective agents, informing them of the arrival of the written or printed copies of the record as the case may be, but it must be borne in mind his so doing is a matter of courtesy, and is not a matter of duty. After the printed copies have been received at the Council office, the respective agents will, on application, be allowed, free of charge, five copies each.

Should a certified written copy of the record be forwarded to the Council office, the first step is for the appellant to bespeak a copy of it; this he does in the following form :—

IN THE PRIVY COUNCIL.

State this shortly.

In the matter of the appeal of

Appeal No. ——, of 186—.

Fill in number.

I hereby request the Registrar of the Privy Council to cause the transcript record in the above-named appeal, or such parts thereof as are necessary for the hearing of the same, to be copied and printed, and I engage on behalf of the appellant to pay for such copy and printing at the rate of 1s. per brief sheet of stationers' copying, and at the Government price of printing the same.

A. B.,

Appellant's solicitor or agent.

Upon this request—a lithographic copy of which can be obtained at the Council office—being left at the Council office, a copy is at once put in hand, and is furnished to the appellant's agent on payment of the same at the rate of 1s. per stationers' brief sheet.

The time this copy takes making will depend on the length of the record, and as great care is taken in making this copy, considerable time often elapses before it is ready.

The appellant's agent has then to go through the copy furnished him, and make up his mind as to which of the documents he requires to be printed. He has power to object to any portion of the record which appears to him to be unnecessary for the hearing of the appeal being printed, and it is his duty in cases in which portions of the record contain merely formal or irrelevant matter to offer to exclude it from the printed record. So soon as the appellant's agent has made up his own mind as to what portions of the record he wishes to have printed, he forwards the copy to the respondent's agents, intimating the portions (if any) he wishes to have excluded from the printed copy. It then becomes the duty of the respondent's agent in his turn to go through the copy, and should he be of opinion that some of the portions that the appellant's agent wishes to exclude are necessary to his defence of the appeal, he has a right to refuse to allow the transcript to be printed without them.

It may be as well to point out in this place the meaning and origin of the word Appendix as mentioned in the 4th rule of the Orders in Council of 13th June, 1853, (page 150). Many years ago, when the cost for printing was a more serious matter than at present, only so much of the record was printed as was absolutely necessary. It was, however, found that in the printed cases lodged by each party many documents other than those that were printed had to be referred to, and as this caused considerable confusion, by an Order in Council of 3rd July, 1838, it was ordered that all printed cases of appeals which have an appendix annexed, should be accompanied with a joint appendix of the documents or other papers referred to in the cases of the parties, and that neither party should be entitled to set down his case for hearing upon lodging a separate appendix, unless accompanied by an affidavit of the refusal of the opposite party to unite in a joint appendix. This rule, though apparently not repealed, may be taken to be obsolete, it being very seldom, if ever, necessary in either the appellant's or respondent's case to refer to any documents other than those printed in the transcript of the record ; as a matter of practice, the only appendix to the record is the index to the documents printed, and a reference to the pages at which they will be found so printed.

Any refusal to allow portions of the certified copy record to be omitted from the printed one has to be at the risk of the party refusing, who may possibly be visited with the costs occasioned by such unnecessary printing. It often happens that there are more respondents than one, and that their interests not being identical, they appear by separate solicitors. When this is so, each solicitor is entitled to see the record, and all have equal power of objection to the exclusion or introduction in the printed record of unnecessary matter.

It is impossible to lay down any rule as to what documents ought not to be printed, as each case must of necessity differ ; and it

c

would appear advisable, even at the risk of costs, to print too much than to print too little.

In a case some short time back, in which the record had been printed in India, a number of rent receipts, being all in one form, were printed; their lordships, on the hearing of this appeal, made some very strong observations on the waste of money occasioned by so much unnecessary matter being printed.

After the copy of the record has been perused by the agents of all the parties to the appeal, it is then returned by the appellant's agent to the Privy Council office, and is then printed by Her Majesty's Printers. The costs of this printing may be taken to be about 1*l.* 15*s.* to 2*l.* for each printed folio sheet (a folio sheet containing four printed pages).

There are generally seventy-six lines in each page printed in **England**; whilst in India the practice appears to be never to print more than sixty lines in each page, and in many cases even a less number.

The average number of folios per printed page is fifteen, making sixty per printed folio sheet.

After the copy has been set up in type, the solicitors on both sides attend at the Council office for the purpose of examining the printed copy with the original certified one. For this attendance they are each allowed to charge two guineas per diem, and it is considered a fair day's work to examine twenty-four printed pages.

The solicitors are allowed a further fee of one guinea for correcting each foreign or Indian folio proof-sheet, and 10s. 6d. each folio sheet for correcting all other proofs.

When the record is long it is impossible to set up the whole of it in type at once. The proof sheets are examined with the original certified copy as they come from the printers, and the corrected proof sheets are then again examined, to see that the necessary alterations have been made. The solicitors on each side are allowed to charge as between party and party for any reasonable correspondence and attendances respecting these examinations.

By section 5 of Order in Council of 13th June, 1853 (vide page 151) it is directed that an appeal shall stand dismissed, without further order in case of appeals, from places east of the Cape of Good Hope or territories of the

East India Company, unless the appellant
or his agent take effectual steps within six
months after the arrival and registration of
the copy record to prosecute the appeal,
and in cases of appeals from any other
parts of Her Majesty's dominions abroad,
the time is limited to three months after
the arrival and registration of such copy
record.

The act of applying for a copy of the certified copy of the appeal when the record is
sent home unprinted, or of entering an appearance when the record is forwarded
printed, is a sufficient effectual act within
the meaning of this rule.

It is the duty of the appellant's agent to
prepare an index to the documents in the
printed record before he returns the copy
to the Privy Council office for the purpose of being printed. He will find an
index of all the papers contained in the
certified copy forwarded from the colonial
court.

There is no special rule laid down respecting the preparation or form of this index.
The following appears to be the best for
reference, and is the one usually adopted.
This index is prepared by the appellant's

agent, and is usually called a scheme for printing.

Marginal Number.	Number of Document on Record.	Description of Document.	Page.

The marginal number is the consecutive number of the document in the order in which it is printed. This number is placed in the left-hand margin of the record when printed.

The number of the document on record is the number attached to the document in the colonial court.

The description is generally taken from the index prepared in the colony.

The page is the page in the printed record.

ENTERING APPEARANCE.

WHEN the appellant's agent has received information from his colonial correspondent that liberty to appeal has been granted by the court below, he should at once give a notice of his appearance to the Registrar of the Judicial Committee. So soon as the respondent's agent becomes aware of the appeal he should also give a similar notice.

The following form may be adopted :

(*Address*).

(*Date*).

To

The Registrar of **Her** Majesty's Most Honourable Privy Council.

Name of court.

On appeal from

BETWEEN

Appellant,

Full title.

and

Respondent.

Appeal No. ——, of 186—.

SIR,

I shall be obliged by your noting my appearance herein on behalf of the above-named (appellant or respondent, as case may be).

Yours obediently,

——, (Solicitor or agent)

(For appellant or respondent).

Care must be **taken** in wording **this** notice to bring **it** within the rule laid down by their Lordships in the following circular :

Privy Council Office,

4th Feb., 1869.

SIR,

I am directed by the Lords of the Judicial Committee to inform you that when a solicitor or agent enters an appearance for a respondent in an appeal to

Her Majesty **in Council, their** lordships **require that** the names **of all the** respondents **should be fully** and correctly **stated in the notice, in** writing, and also the **court appealed from, the date of the decree appealed from, and (in Indian** cases**) the number of the** suit.

I am instructed **by their** lordships not **to receive** notices of appearance **in** which these particulars are omitted.

(Signed)   HENRY REEVE,

Registrar, P. C.

Considerable difficulty may in many cases be experienced by agents in England **in** order strictly **to** comply **with the above rule,** as **it is** sometimes **next to impossible to** make out **from the** instructions forwarded from the colony, and in some cases even from the record **itself,** who are the actual respondents; the title of the cause is often shortly stated **as** being against So-and-so, respondent, and others. It also now appears from a recent decision **of** the Judicial Committee that it is the duty of the respondent's **agent to** attend from time to time at the **Privy** Council office to search **the** various records that arrive, to find out if the particular one of the appeal to which he appears is among **the** number.

When the agent is instructed to appear in an appeal to which there are several respondents, and he is not certain whether he is authorised to appear for one or all of them, but is in other respects able to comply with the directions contained in the above letter, it is advisable for him to give notice of his appearance on behalf of those respondents for whom he is certain that he is instructed to act. He can then write to his colonial agent for further particulars.

PETITION OF APPEAL.

THE appellant having appeared, and the record having been printed, the next step is the preparation of the petition of appeal.

This petition is prepared by the appellant's agent, and is always settled by the junior counsel. In cases in which the appeal is of right, this petition may be in the form appended at pages 137 and 140.

It has to be entitled in the Privy Council, and care must be taken that the names of all the appellants and respondents appear in the title of the appeal. In cases in which an appellant is preparing this petition of appeal, before the respondent or all the respondents have appeared, care must be taken that he only makes such of the respondents parties as appeared in the Court below; the addition of a respondent who does not appear will possibly put the appellant to the cost and delay of citing the respondent so named by him to appear, as pointed out page 36.

The petition is engrossed on brief paper, and is lodged at the Council office; it does not require any verification, nor is it necessary that it should be signed by counsel.

No order is drawn up on a petition when the appellant has an appeal as of right; the appeal is admitted as a matter of course; the fee for lodging is 1*l.* 1*s.*

If the respondent has appeared, he is served with a copy of the petition.

In no case is the petition of appeal to be printed.

In cases in which special leave to appeal has to be applied for, the petition must be verified by affidavit. The usual and most concise form of verification is the addition of a short affidavit at the end of the petition; this may be in the following form :—

c 3

State shortly the grounds upon which belief is founded.

I, ——, of ——, from a perusal of —— verily believe that the matters in the said petition are true.

Sworn at the Privy Council Office,
Whitehall, this ——— day of
———.

Before me, ———

The verification is, however, sometimes by a separate affidavit, in which case the following form may be used:—

IN THE PRIVY COUNCIL.

Name of court.

On appeal from

BETWEEN

Appellant,

Full title.

and

Respondent.

I, ——, of ——, solicitor or agent for the above-named appellant, make oath and say,

That to the best of my knowledge, information, and belief, the allegations and statements contained in the petition of the above-named appellant, for special leave to appeal against an order of the High Court of Judicature at Fort William, in Bengal, rejecting a petition of review, are true.

That I received through the post, from the vakeel of the appellant in India, copies of the proceedings and documents referred to in the said petition, which I have since deposited in the

Registry of the Judicial Committee of the Privy Council for reference if needful.

Sworn at the Privy Council Office,
Whitehall, the —— day of
——, 186—.

Before me, ——

It will be noticed that the title of this affidavit differs from the title of an ordinary petition for special leave, vide page 143; this is owing to the petition, in support of which it is made, being for special leave to appeal against an order made by the lower Court in a cause already depending in appeal before the Privy Council; in other cases the affidavit must be entitled in the same manner as the petition for special leave.

When an appearance has been entered by a respondent, a copy of the petition for special leave, as well as of the affidavit in support, must be furnished to his agent.

A brief is given to counsel to attend and move in the terms of the prayer of the petition; and if the prayer be granted, the Committees report to Her Majesty, as well as the Order in Council, are then drawn up, the latter being handed to the petitioner's agent, who transmits it to his correspondent.

When the petition is dismissed, no committee order dismissing it is drawn up unless an application for one is made.

A respondent who obtains information that a petition for special leave is about to be presented, ought to enter an appearance, his agent will then be served with a copy of the petition, and will be entitled to be heard by counsel when the motion is made.

When special leave to appeal is granted, the costs of the application are usually costs in the appeal.

PROCEEDINGS FOR COMPELLING A RESPONDENT TO APPEAR.

THE appellant's agent having prepared and lodged the petition of appeal, and the respondent having failed to appear, has then to take steps for calling on the respondent to appear, so as to enable him, in case he fails to do so, to prosecute his appeal *ex parte.*

To enable him to do this, it is not necessary, when the appeal is printed in England, that he should bring in his own printed case ; it is sufficient, to entitle him to proceed for

such purpose, that he should have printed
the record and lodged his petition of appeal ;
having done these two acts, he then presents
a petition asking for an order for a summons
to issue calling on the respondent to appear
within two months from the service of the
order. An order on this petition is obtained
as of course.

The following may be the form of a
petition for such order :—

IN THE PRIVY COUNCIL.

On appeal from   Name of
                                         court.
    BETWEEN

                              Appellant,

            and   Full title.

                              Respondent.

        Appeal No. ——, of 186—.

    To
The Judicial Committee of Her Majesty's Most
Honourable Privy Council.

The humble petition of the above-named appel-
    lant,

    SHEWETH,
That this is an appeal from a decision of ——,
dated the —— day of ——, 186—.

That the record has been printed in ——, and

has been duly transmitted to the Registrar of Her
Majesty's Most Honourable Privy Council (a).

That, on the —— day of —— now last past
your petitioner lodged his petition of appeal, and
on the —— day of —— following, brought in his
printed case.

That the respondent has not caused any appearance to be entered on his behalf, and your petitioner
has not received any notice or intimation of any
person being appointed to act as the agent of such
respondent in England, nor is your petitioner aware
if the said respondent intends appearing to this
appeal.

> Your petitioner, therefore, humbly prays
> your lordships to fix a day for hearing
> his said appeal, and for an order direct-
> ing the usual summons to issue calling
> on the said respondent to appear forth-
> with.

> And your petitioner will ever pray, &c.

The following is a copy of the order made
on this petition, and of the summons that
issues with it :—

(a) *Or*, That your petitioner having caused the record
in this appeal to be printed, on the —— day of ——
lodged his petition of appeal.

At the Council Chamber, Whitehall,
the ——— day of ——— 186—.

By the Judicial Committee of the Privy Council.

Whereas Her Majesty was pleased by her Order in Council of the ——— of ——— to refer unto this Committee the humble petition and appeal of ———.

And whereas a motion was this day made to their lordships praying that a day may be appointed for hearing the said appeal, and also praying in regard thereto, as no appearance hath been entered for the respondent to the said appeal, that the usual summons may be issued requiring his appearance thereto : Their lordships are thereupon pleased to order, and it is hereby ordered, that the said appeal be heard at this Committee on the ——— day of ——— next, at twelve o'clock at noon, and that the usual summons be affixed on the Royal Exchange and elsewhere in the usual manner, requiring the said respondent to enter an appearance forthwith to the said appeal, and to come prepared to be heard thereupon by his counsel learned in the law, on the said ——— day of ——— next.

———, Registrar, P. C.

Council Office, Whitehall,

——— of ———, 186—.

Whereas the Judicial Committee of the Privy Council have appointed to meet in the Council

Chamber at Whitehall, on ——— the ——— day of ——— next, at twelve o'clock at noon, to hear the appeal of ———.

And whereas no appearance hath been hitherto entered for the said respondent to the said appeal, these are therefore to give notice to the said respondent that he do forthwith enter an appearance to the said appeal, and come prepared to be heard thereupon by his counsel learned in the law, on the said ——— day of ——— next.

———, Registrar, P. C.

The appellant's agent must fix up a copy of the summons at the Royal Exchange, and also at Lloyd's Coffee House.

If the respondent does not cause an appearance to be entered within the time mentioned in the summons, which time is usually fixed at two months from the date of its issue, the appellant's agent then makes an affidavit of the posting of the summons as directed, and applies upon another petition for a peremptory order calling upon the respondent to enter an appearance within six weeks from the service of such order.

The following are forms of petition and affidavit that may be used :—

IN THE PRIVY COUNCIL.

On appeal from

Name of court.

BETWEEN

Appellant,

and

Full title.

Respondent.

Appeal No. ——, of 186—.

To

The Judicial Committee of Her Majesty's Most Honourable Privy Council.

The humble petition of the above-named appellant,

SHEWETH,

That on the —— day of —— your lordships were pleased, on the application of your petitioner, to appoint ——, the —— day of —— next, for the hearing of this appeal, and your lordships further directed the usual summons to issue calling upon the respondent forthwith to appear, to be fixed on the Royal Exchange, and elsewhere, in the usual manner.

That on the —— day of —— your petitioner, in pursuance of your lordships' said direction, caused a true copy of the said summons to be affixed in a conspicuous place at the Royal Exchange, in the City of London, and he also caused another true copy of the said summons to be affixed in a conspicuous place at Lloyd's Coffee House, in the said City of London, but the said respondent has neglected to enter or cause an appearance to be entered for him to this appeal.

> Your petitioner humbly prays that your lordships will grant him the usual peremptory order, directing the above-named respondent to enter an appearance within six weeks from the service of the order to be made herein.

And your petitioner will ever pray, &c.

IN THE PRIVY COUNCIL.

Name of court.

On appeal from

BETWEEN

Appellant,

Full title.

and

Respondent.

I, ——, of ——, in the City of London, (solicitor or agent) for the above-named appellant, make oath and say,

That on the —— day of ——, now last past, I caused a copy of the summons, a true copy whereof is hereunto annexed, to be affixed in a conspicuous place at the Royal Exchange, in the City of London, and on the said —— day of —— now last past I also caused another true copy of the said summons to be affixed in a conspicuous place at Lloyd's Coffee House, in the said City of London.

Sworn at the Privy Council Office, Whitehall, this —— day of ——, 186—. (*a*)

Before me, ——

(*a*) All jurats are engrossed on the left hand side.

The following is the order made on this petition :—

At the Council Chamber, Whitehall,
—— day of ——.

By the Judicial Committee of the Privy Council.

Upon a motion this day made to their lordships for a peremptory order requiring —— to appear to the appeal of ——, from ——, their lordships are pleased peremptorily to order that the said respondent do enter an appearance to the said appeal within six weeks from the date hereof, otherwise their lordships will proceed to hear the said appeal *ex parte.*

——, Registrar, P. C.

This order must also be affixed in the same manner as hereinbefore pointed out in reference to the summons.

If the respondent fails to obey this last-mentioned order and to appear within the six weeks thereby limited, the appellant's agent again applies to the Judicial Committee on petition, supported by affidavit, for an order to set down the appeal for hearing *ex parte.*

The following are forms of this petition and affidavit :—

IN THE PRIVY COUNCIL.

Name of
court. On appeal from

BETWEEN

Appellant,

Full title.   and

Respondent.

Appeal No. ——, of 186—.

To

The Judicial Committee of Her Majesty's Most Honourable Privy Council.

The humble petition of the above-named appellant,

SHEWETH,

That on the —— day of ——, now last past, your petitioner obtained a peremptory order from your lordships, directing the respondent to bring in his case within six weeks from the date of such order.

That on the —— day of —— your petitioner caused true copies of the said order to be affixed in conspicuous places at the Royal Exchange, and also at Lloyd's Coffee House in the City of London, but the said respondent has neglected to cause an appearance to be entered for him.

> Your petitioner therefore humbly prays your lordships to allow his appeal to be set down for hearing *ex parte*.

And your petitioner will ever pray, &c.

In the Privy Council.

On appeal from

Between

                                        Appellant,
                    and
                                        Respondent.

Appeal No. ——, of 186—.

I, ——, of ——, in the City of London, (solicitor or agent) for the above-named appellant, make oath and say,

That on the —— day of ——, now last past, I caused a true copy of the order, a true copy whereof is hereunto annexed, to be affixed in a conspicuous place in the Royal Exchange, in the City of London, and on the said —— day of —— I also caused another true copy of the said order to be affixed in a conspicuous place at Lloyd's Coffee House, in the said City of London.

Sworn at the Privy Council Office,
    Whitehall, this —— day of
    ——, 186—.

                    Before me, ——

No formal order is drawn up upon this petition, but the prayer is granted as of course, and the case is set down for hearing *ex parte*.

Notwithstanding a case being set down *ex parte*, owing to the non-appearance of a respondent, it is open to such respondent to appear within any reasonable time before

the hearing, in which case the appeal goes
on in the usual manner. A respondent who
appears at the eleventh hour should lose no
time in lodging his printed case ; if a further
default takes place, he might be precluded
from appearing at all at the hearing ; even
if this were not so, he would certainly be
saddled with costs.

AS TO PREPARATION AND LODGING CASES ON BEHALF OF THE APPELLANT AND RESPONDENT.

THE petition of appeal having been duly
lodged, each party has to prepare a case.
Should there be more than one respondent,
and separate appearances entered, each respondent can prepare a separate case ; but if
the Lords of the Committee, when the appeal is heard, are of opinion that one joint
case on behalf of all the respondents would
have been sufficient, they may refuse to allow
the costs of the preparation of more than one
case.

Neither party is allowed to see his adversary's case till he has lodged his own.

The case is drafted by the junior counsel,
and it is in most cases settled in conference

between the senior and the junior; after being so settled, it is printed by the respective agents.

The case should be printed on folio paper of the same size as the record; as a rule, it contains from fifty to sixty lines in each printed page; references should, whenever possible, be made in the right-hand margin of the printed case to the page and line of the record that supports each allegation: thus, "Record, page 60, line 10."

It is always as well to have 100 copies struck off by the printer. The cost for printing these 100 copies is the same as the cost of printing the record (*vide* page 4), and averages from 35s. to 2l. per folio page.

Great care is necessary in framing a case; it ought to be drawn, having strict regard to the facts appearing on the record, and it is most advisable that all doubtful arguments should be excluded. It must be remembered that neither the appellant nor respondent is precluded by his case from the argument of any point not appearing on the face of it. The chief object of these cases is to present in a concise form to the Judicial Committee the arguments of each side.

After the case is printed, forty copies must be lodged with the Registrar of the Privy Council.

So soon as either party is in a position to lodge his case, it is usual for him to give a notice of this fact to his adversary, and to make an appointment to meet and exchange cases; but if this notice is not attended to, it rests with the party giving it to take the proceedings pointed out at page 49 to force the opposite side to bring in his case.

It is usual to exchange ten copies on each side.

AS TO PREPARATION OF A JOINT CASE ON BEHALF OF APPELLANT AND RESPONDENT.

By the 6th rule of the Order in Council of 13th June, 1853 (*vide* page 152), it is directed that the appeal may be submitted to the Judicial Committee in the form of a special case; but this can only be done when the matter of appeal turns exclusively on a question of law, and it must then be done with the sanction of the Registrar. The rule further provides that nothing is to prevent the Committee, if they so wish, from ordering the full discussion of the whole case. The Registrar has also power to call the parties before him, and he then reports to the Committee.

This Order in Council is very seldom acted upon, there being so few cases in which the question at issue turns exclusively on a point of law; and as it would be in almost all cases necessary for counsel to attend on the argument of the special case, it is very questionable if there would be much, if any, saving of cost by adopting this rule and agreeing to a special case.

PROCEEDINGS TO COMPEL THE OPPOSITE PARTY TO BRING IN HIS CASE.

WHEN either party has lodged his printed case, he is then in a position to take steps to force the opposite party also to lodge his printed case; his first step towards this end is to present a petition at the Council office. stating the position of the appeal, and praying for an order for the party in default to bring in his printed case. The following is the form of such a petition; it can, if necessary, be altered so as to meet the circumstances of each case :—

D

IN THE PRIVY COUNCIL.

Name of court.

On appeal from

BETWEEN

Appellant,

and

Respondent.

Appeal No. ——, of 186—.

To

The Judicial Committee of Her Majesty's Most Honourable Privy Council.

Full title.

Appellant or respondent, as the case may be.

The humble petition of the above-named ——

SHEWETH,

State name of court and date of decision appealed from.

That this is an appeal from a decision of ——, dated the —— day of ——, 18—.

If record printed in England, leave this out.

That the record has been printed in ——, and copies have been duly transmitted to the Registrar of Her Majesty's Most Honourable Privy Council.

Or appellant, as the case may be.

That the respondent entered an appearance on the —— day of —— last, through ——, of ——, his (solicitor or agent).

If respondent, leave out words " lodged his petition of appeal."

Or appellant.

That your petitioner has duly lodged his petition of appeal, and has brought in his case, but the respondent has failed to bring in his case.

Your petitioner, therefore, humbly prays your lordships to grant him the usual order calling upon the respondent forth- ^{Or appel-lant.}with to bring in his case.

And your petitioner will ever pray, &c.

The following is a copy of the order made on this petition :—

At the Council Chamber, Whitehall,
the —— day of ——, 186—.

BY THE JUDICIAL COMMITTEE OF THE PRIVY COUNCIL.

Upon a motion this day made to their lordships for an order requiring the (appellant or respondent, as the case may be,) in the appeal of —— against ^{Title of appeal.} ——, from ——, to bring in (his) printed case. ^{Name of court.} Their lordships are pleased to order that the said (appellant or respondent, as the case may be,) do deliver (his or their) printed case within one month from the service of this order.

——, Registrar, P. C.

If the party served with this order fails to bring in his printed case within the month mentioned in it, at the expiration of such time, on the application of the agent who obtained such order, another order will issue calling upon the defaulter peremptorily to bring in his printed case within fourteen days from the service of such last-mentioned order.

D 2

This order is likewise obtained on a petition, which may be in the following form :—

In the Privy Council.

On appeal from

Between

Appellant,

and

Respondent.

Appeal No. ——, of 186—.

To

The Judicial Committee of Her Majesty's Most Honourable Privy Council.

The humble petition of the above-named ——

Sheweth,

That on the —— day of ——, your petitioner obtained an order from your lordships directing the

—— in the above appeal to bring in his printed case within one month from the service of such order.

That your petitioner, on the —— day of ——, caused the said order to be served upon ——, as

(solicitor or agent) for the said ——, but the said —— has failed to comply with the terms of such order.

Your petitioner, therefore, humbly prays your lordships to grant him the usual peremptory order directing the —— to _{Appellant or respondent.} bring in his printed case within fourteen days from the service of the order to be made hereon.

And your petitioner will ever pray, &c.

The following is a copy of an order made on such a petition :—

At the Council Chamber, Whitehall,
the —— day of ——, 186—.

BY THE JUDICIAL COMMITTEE OF THE PRIVY
COUNCIL.

Upon a motion this day made to their lordships for a peremptory order requiring the —— in the appeal of —— against ——, from ——, to bring in —— printed case. Their lordships are pleased peremptorily to order that the said —— do deliver —— printed case within a fortnight from the service of this order, otherwise their lordships will proceed to hear the said appeal *ex parte*.

——, Registrar, P. C.

The petition upon which this order is obtained must be supported by an affidavit of the service of the former order; this affidavit may be in the following form :—

IN THE PRIVY COUNCIL.

Name of court.

On appeal from

BETWEEN

Appellant,

Full title.

and

Respondent.

Full name and description.

I, ——, of ——, in the City of London, a clerk in the employ of —— of ——, make oath and say, as follows :—

That I am a clerk in the employ of the above-named ——, who is the (solicitor or agent) in *Appellant or respondent.* England on behalf of the above-named ——.

Name and address.

That Mr. ——, of ——, has caused an appearance to be entered in his name as the (solicitor or agent) for the above-named ——.

That on the —— day of ——, now last past, I served the order, a true copy whereof is hereunto annexed, on the said ——, as such (solicitor or *Name.* agent) as aforesaid, by delivering to ——, a clerk in the employ of the said ——, at his said office, a true copy of the said order, and at the same time producing the original of such order.

Sworn at the Privy Council Office,
    Whitehall, this —— day of
    ——, 186—.

Before me, ——

This affidavit is sworn before the Registrar at the Council office, and is then lodged there. The fee for lodging it is 1*l.* 1*s.*

If at the expiration of the fourteen days named in this peremptory order, the party against whom it is made fails to obey it, the party who has obtained the order, upon making an affidavit of service and presenting a petition, is entitled to have the cause set down for hearing *ex parte*.

The following are forms of this petition and affidavit:—

IN THE PRIVY COUNCIL.

On appeal from

Name of court.

BETWEEN

Appellant,

and

Full title.

Respondent.

Appeal No. ——, of 186—.

To

The Judicial Committee of Her Majesty's Most Honourable Privy Council.

The humble petition of the above-named ——

Appellant or respondent.

SHEWETH,

That on the —— day of ——, now last past, your petitioner obtained an order from your lordships, peremptorily directing the —— to bring in his case within fourteen days from the service of such order.

Appellant or respondent.

That your petitioner on the —— day of ——

caused the said order to be served upon ——

(solicitor or agent), for the said ——, but the said
—— has failed to comply with the terms of such
order.

Your petitioner therefore humbly prays your
lordships to allow this appeal to be set
down for hearing *ex parte*.

IN THE PRIVY COUNCIL.

Name of
court.

On appeal from

BETWEEN

Appellant,

Full title.

and

Respondent.

Appeal No. ——, of 186—.

Name and
address.
Solicitor's
or agent's
name and
address.

I, ——, of ——, in the City of London, a clerk
in the employ of Mr. ——, of ——, make oath
and say, as follows :—

That I am a clerk in the employ of the above-
named ——, who is the (solicitor or agent) in
England on behalf of the above-named ——.

That on the —— day of ——, Mr. ——, of
——, caused an appearance to be entered in his
name, as the (solicitor or agent) for the above-

Appellant or
respondent.

named ——.

That on the —— day of ——, now last past,
I served the order, a true copy whereof is hereunto annexed, on the said Mr. ——, as such
(solicitor or agent) as aforesaid, by delivering

to ——, a clerk in the employ of the said Mr. ——, at his said office, a true copy of the said order, and at the same time producing the original of such order.

Sworn at the Privy Council Office,
    Whitehall, this —— day of
    ——, 186—.
             Before me, ——

No order is drawn up on this petition, but the appeal is put in the cause list as of course.

After an appeal has been set down for hearing *ex parte*, it is open to the defaulting party, at any reasonable time before the day fixed for hearing the appeal, to bring in his printed case, and if he does so in sufficient time to enable copies to be distributed among the members of the Committee, the appeal will go on in all respects as if the case had been lodged in due course.

It appears that a printed case will be received at any time previous to the actual hearing, but a delay may lay the defaulting party open to the costs of a postponement of the hearing. Should a postponement be necessary, an application for it must be made to the Committee when the cause is in the paper.

It does not appear that there is any rule

making a party in default pay the costs occasioned by his default, except as herein pointed out.

CONSOLIDATION OF APPEALS.

EACH party who feels aggrieved by a decree should appeal from that portion he complains of. It often happens that both plaintiff and defendant in the Court below appeal from the same decree, in which case there are cross appeals. When there are cross appeals an order is usually made to consolidate them. The application for an order to consolidate two appeals can be made by either party at any time, and must be on petition to Her Majesty, and has to be moved by counsel. This order is only made when the same parties who are appellants in one case are respondents in the other, and *vice versâ*.

DISMISSAL OF APPEAL PREVIOUS TO HEARING.

BY the Order in Council of 13th June, 1853, an appeal dismisses itself in default of the appellant or his agent taking effectual steps for the prosecution of the appeal within three or six months, as mentioned at page 152.

Entering appearance, bespeaking copy of the record, or lodging petition of appeal, is a sufficient effectual step to prevent this rule operating.

After the appeal is once admitted there does not appear to be any time limited within which further steps have to be taken to prevent the appeal being dismissed for want of prosecution.

The appeal once being admitted, it is open to the respondent to force the appeal to a hearing (*ante*, page 49), and it is equally open to the appellant to bring on his appeal (*ex parte*, page 36), so there is no occasion for any rule in this respect. However, after an appeal has been delayed for a considerable time it is usual for their lordships to direct a notice to issue calling on the appellant to proceed within a given time, failing which the appeal stands dismissed.

ABATEMENT AND REVIVOR.

AN appeal often during its progress abates by reason of the death or other change in the status of the appellant. When this happens, it must be revived.

It is also necessary, in certain cases, when a respondent dies, that the appeal should be revived against his representatives.

Death, bankruptcy, marriage, and lunacy are some of the causes of abatement. Each case is, however, governed by the law of the country appealed from.

After the appeal is once admitted, the application for revivor should, in all cases, be to Her Majesty in Council. In many colonial and foreign Courts application is frequently made to such Courts even after the appeal has been admitted for its revivor, but it is submitted that such practice is wrong, though the Judicial Committee may have to refer to the lower Court to decide who are the representatives of an abated appellant or respondent.

The application is made on a petition, which is usually verified, and is moved by counsel.

SETTLEMENT PREVIOUS TO HEARING.

IT is open to the parties, after appeal, to abandon it, or to come to a compromise, and upon a proper petition being presented the Privy Council will pass any orders which may be necessary for effecting any *bonâ fide* compromise, or it will grant liberty for an application to be made to the lower Court.

These applications must, in all cases, be made to Her Majesty in Council by petition, and are moved by counsel.

The fact of a respondent retiring from the appeal does not entitle the appellant to an order in his favour, the appeal will still have to proceed *ex parte*.

BINDING UP COPIES FOR JUDGES.

IT is the duty of the appellant's agent, before the hearing of the appeal, to bind up in separate volumes ten copies of the proceedings in the Privy Council; these copies are bound up for the use of the judges. Each volume will consist of a print of the record, and all the printed cases lodged on behalf of the various parties who appear on the appeal.

These volumes should be bound up in the following order :—*First*, the appellant's case ; *second*, the respondent's case or cases ; and *third*, the record.

It is also advisable to have a label printed stating the name of the Court appealed from, the short title of the cause, the number of the appeal, and the appellant's agent's name; the labels are stuck on the cover of each volume.

On application by the appellant's agent at the Council office, ten complete copies of the proceedings will be handed to him for the purpose of being bound together; the costs of this binding will be allowed on taxation, as between party and party.

The respondent's agent, as a rule, also binds up three copies—two for his counsel, and one for use. These copies will not be furnished by the Council office. The cost of binding these copies will be allowed on taxation, as between party and party.

SUMMONING THE PARTIES TO ATTEND HEARING.

THE cause having been set down on the list will in most cases be heard according to its position in such list; but sometimes, towards the end of the sittings, a short appeal is taken out of its turn with the object of reducing the number of remanet appeals; also in certain cases, on the application of counsel, a day is fixed for hearing some particular appeal.

A notice, called a summons, is always sent to the agents on both sides, informing them of the day appointed for the hearing of the appeal; this notice is delivered at the agent's office by a messenger of the Council office.

This summons is usually, but not always, sent out two clear days before the day fixed for hearing the appeal.

ON THE ARGUMENT OF THE APPEAL.

BOTH parties having been summoned to appear, the argument is opened by the senior counsel for the appellant; he is then followed by his junior; the respondent's two counsel are then heard in answer, the appellant's counsel having the right of reply.

The Judicial Committee take no notice of any rules of procedure of the Court appealed from, as being binding upon them respecting the procedure of the appeal in England.

When there are several appellants and respondents who have different interests, and who have appeared by separate agents in the same appeal, whenever possible, such several appellants or respondents should be represented by the same two counsel—the cost of employment of more counsel than are absolutely necessary being visited on the parties offending; but when the appeals are separate ones, though consolidated, there appears to be a right to employ different sets of counsel in each appeal.

It is advisable, in any appeal in which a question has arisen between the agents as to the employment of joint counsel, to have the offer and refusal in writing, and to embody the facts in an affidavit, so that it can, if necessary, be used at the argument. A Judicial Committee has full power to hear any affidavit made on the appeal read. It must be always borne in mind that the rule is that the matter contained in the record, and the record alone, is the subject of appeal; but in cases such as petitions for special leave to appeal, and also in support of any application respecting matters that have arisen after the record has come to this country, affidavits are usually made and received from both sides.

It must be remembered that a Judicial Committee has unlimited power in the way

of procedure ; in some cases it will, even
after the argument is closed, summon
counsel again to attend to argue some stated
point, and will sometimes summon witnesses before it to clear up points of doubt.
In any such extraordinary cases, agents
must be guided by the facts of the case, and
the terms of the summons, in deciding how
the various interests are to be represented
at the re-hearing.

JUDGMENT.

THE judgment of the Court is delivered
by one judge only; the judgment need not
be unanimous, a majority being sufficient.

A shorthand note is taken of the judgment, and is generally corrected by the judge
who delivered it ; it is then printed ; each
party has delivered to him, gratis, on application, a reasonable number of copies.

After judgment is delivered, a report is
drawn up by the Committee and submitted
to the Queen for approval at the first (a)
Cabinet Council held after its receipt.   The

(a) A Cabinet Council is usually held within one month
after the date of the committee report.

Order in Council which recites the report is then drawn up, and it is handed to the agent of the successful party on his application at the Council office. It then becomes his duty to transmit the original order of her Majesty in Council to his colonial agent.

COSTS.

The following is a schedule of authorised fees allowed to solicitors conducting appeals before the Judicial Committee of the Privy Council under her Majesty's Orders in Council of the 11th August, 1842, and the 13th June, 1853.

	£	s.	d.
Retainer fee	0	13	4
Perusing official copy of proceedings, allowed at the rate of 6s. 8d. for the perusal of three brief sheets or 25 folios (a)			
Attendances at the Council office, or elsewhere, on ordinary business, such as to enter an appeal or an appearance, to make a search, to lodge a petition or affidavit, or to retain counsel	0	10	0

(a) When record is printed abroad the solicitor is allowed one guinea for each printed folio sheet for perusing.

	£	s.	d.
Attending at Privy Council office to examine printed copy of transcript with the original, per diem (a)	2	2	0
Instructions for petition of appeal	0	10	0
Drawing petition or case, per folio	0	2	0
Copying, per folio,	0	0	6
Drawing small petitions for orders, &c. (b)	0	10	0
Instructions for case	1	0	0
Attending consultation	1	0	0
Correcting proof sheets per printed sheet (c)	0	10	6
Correcting foreign or Indian proof sheets per printed sheet (d)	1	1	0
Attending at Council Chamber on a petition	1	6	8
Attending Council Chamber all day on an appeal not called on	2	6	8
Attending a hearing	3	6	8
Attending a judgment	1	6	8
Sessions fee (for legal year) equal to four term fees	3	3	0
Attending taxation	2	2	0
Attending at Council office on the drawing up of minutes for Council report	1	1	0

(a) The examination of twenty-four printed pages is considered a fair average day's work.

(b) No instructions allowed.

(c) Four printed pages go to the folio sheet, which ought to contain sixty folios of words.

(d) French or Dutch records fall within this description. The record is considered foreign when it contains foreign names and expressions.

By section 1 of the Order in Council of
13th June, 1853, page 147, the appellant is
entitled to recover against the respondent
the cost of his appeal, unless the Judicial
Committee think fit otherwise to direct;
formerly a successful appellant had to pay
his own costs in any event.

When an appeal is dismissed, it is generally dismissed with costs as against the
appellants.

In cases in which costs are given, the fact
of their being so given forms a portion of
the Order in Council; and when given
against an appellant who has obtained
special leave to appeal, they are at once
paid out of the amount deposited in England as security; but when the security has
been deposited abroad, they must be obtained
through the colonial court.

When costs are given to the respondent,
he can recover the amount by an action in
any court having jurisdiction, or by the process of the colonial court.

Only costs actually incurred are allowed.
When an appellant has, owing to the non-
appearance of the respondent, printed the
record alone, the respondent, should he
afterwards come in and appear, will not be

allowed any fees connected with such printing.

At page 110, *et sequitur*, will be found some precedents of bills of costs. Any other items in the nature of party and party costs incurred during the appeal should be added. A taxation, like all other proceedings in the Privy Council, is not conducted with reference to technical rules, but to the justice of each case.

FEES PAYABLE TO THE PRIVY COUNCIL OFFICE.

The following is the scale of fees taken at the Privy Council office :—

	£	s.	d.
Lodging petition of appeal .	1	1	0
Entering .	1	1	0
Lodging case .	1	1	0
Entering appearance .	0	10	0
Setting down case .	0	10	0
Summons .	0	10	0
Committee report .	1	10	0
Order of Her Majesty in Council (*a*)	3	2	6
Committee **order** .	1	12	6

(*a*) When petition is dismissed **no committee** order or order of her Majesty is **drawn.**

	£	s.	d.
Lodging affidavit	1	1	0
Ditto petition	1	1	0
Notice to attend	0	10	0
Searching books for information of parties	0	10	0
Certificate delivered to parties (a) .	0	10	0
Copies of papers (each side) . . .	0	5	0
Committee references . . .	2	2	0
Lodging caveat (b)	1	1	0
Subpœna to witnesses . . .	0	10	0
Fee for taxation (appeals) . . .	3	3	0
Ditto ditto (petitions) . . .	1	1	0

These fees are generally collected when the appeal is concluded, a note of them being sent to the agents on each side.

APPEAL RULES AND ORDERS IN COUNCIL RELATING TO APPEALS.

THE procedure in an appeal in each case is regulated either by some Act of the colony or dominion from which the appeal is made, or by an Order in Council, or by

(a) Previous to 1853 a certificate of registration of appeal used to be sent to the court appealed from. This practice is now discontinued.

(b) This only applies to patent cases.

instructions issued to the Governor of such colony or dominion.

As before pointed out, *ante*, page 9, the Crown has an inherent right to admit of an appeal; but such right may, by some Act of the Imperial Legislature, have been deputed to the Legislature of the colony or dominion, or have been otherwise limited by Letters Patent or Royal Charter; for instance, the Imperial Legislature has, in the case of South Australia, deputed such authority to the Legislative Council of such colony, and by an Act of its Legislature a Supreme Court is established, and an appeal to the Privy Council is, in certain cases, allowed.

By the Act of the English Parliament, 7 & 8 Vict. c. 69 (6th August, 1844), it is competent to Her Majesty to issue Orders in Council regulating appeals from any judgments, sentences, decrees, or orders of any court of justice within any British colony or possession abroad, although such court should not be a court of errors or appeal within such colony or possession; accordingly, in most cases of appeals from colonies in which there are no courts of errors or appeal, Orders in Council, or what may be termed appeal rules, have been issued; in some cases, but not in all, these rules have been printed, and a copy can be had on application at the Council office. When the rules are not printed, a written copy will be furnished on payment of the charges for it.

It appears unnecessary to set out in the case of each colony the rules at present applicable to appeals, as such rules are frequently altered; and with reference to many of the colonies, it would in some cases require great research, owing to there being so few appeals from the particular colony, correctly to state the present existing rules; a reference however, to the agent in England previous to the institution of the appeal, as pointed out, *ante*, page 8, in cases of difficulty, is the proper course to be adopted.

At page 107, *et sequitur*, will be found a decision respecting the mode of ascertaining the appealable amount; the principle laid down in this decision is equally applicable to appeals from courts other than India.

The following information only relates to appeals from India, Australia, and Canada, being the three principal places from which appeals are made to the Privy Council :—

INDIA.

BENGAL, MADRAS, BOMBAY, AND AGRA.

There are High Courts for each of the Presidencies of Bengal, Madras, and Bombay; there is also a High Court at Agra; each of these High Courts is established by Letters Patent, issued pursuant to the English Act, 24 & 25 Vict. c. 104; the appealable amount is Rs. 10,000 (1000*l*.), or at the discretion of the judges in smaller cases, appeals being regulated by the rules and orders in force at the date the Letters Patent were issued, or which have been issued since such date.

BURMAH.

Under Act 21 of 1863 of the Legislative Council of India, Recorders' Courts are established at Akyab, Rangoon, and Moulmein, and under section 39 of that Act an appeal lies to Her Majesty in Council in suits in which the sum or matter at issue is Rs. 10,000, such appeal being subject to the rules and orders for the time being in force regarding appeals to Her Majesty in Council from the High Court of Judicature at Fort William, in Bengal, in the exercise of its ordinary original civil jurisdiction.

E

Appeals from non-regulation provinces are regulated by Act 2 of 1863 of the Legislative Council of India. The following is a copy of this Act :—

Previous to this Act it was necessary, in all cases of appeals from non-regulation provinces, to obtain special leave to appeal.

Act No. II. of 1863.

(Received the assent of the Governor-General on the 15th January.)

An Act to regulate the admission of Appeals to Her Majesty in Council from certain Judgments and Orders in Provinces not subject to the general regulations.

Preamble.

WHEREAS it is expedient to regulate the admission of appeals to Her Majesty in Council from certain judgments and orders in provinces not subject to the general regulations. It is enacted as follows :—

Admission of appeal.

I. If a party in a suit is desirous of preferring an appeal to Her Majesty in Council from any final judgment, decree, or order made on appeal or revision by the Court of highest civil jurisdiction in any province in British India not subject to the general regulations, or from any such final judgment, decree, or order made in the exercise of original jurisdiction by the said Court, in any case in which the sum or matter at issue is above the amount or value of 10,000 rupees, or in which such judgment, decree, or order shall involve, directly or indirectly, any claim, demand, or question to or respecting property amounting to or of the value of 10,000 rupees, or from any other final judgment, decree, or order made either on appeal or otherwise as aforesaid, when the said Court shall declare that the case is a fit one for appeal to Her Majesty in Council, such Court shall admit such appeal, subject to such rules and orders as shall be in force, or shall from time to time be made in that behalf by Her Majesty in Council, in respect of such appeals from Her Majesty's High Courts of Judicature in British India.

II. It shall further be lawful for such Court, at its discretion, upon the petition of any party who considers himself aggrieved by any preliminary or interlocutory judgment, decree, or order of such Court in any such proceeding as aforesaid (not being of criminal jurisdiction), to grant permission to such party to appeal against the same to Her Majesty in Council, subject to such rules, regulations, and limitations as shall be in force, or as shall from time to time be declared by Her Majesty, respecting appeals from final judgments, decrees, and orders of Her Majesty's said High Courts of Judicature. *Appeal from interlocutory judgments.*

III. On the admission or permission of the appeal by the Court as hereinbefore provided, the Court shall forthwith cause notice to be given to the other party, that the appellant has preferred an appeal to Her Majesty in Council. *Notice of appeal to the other party.*

IV. The Court, if applied to, may either order *Court may either en-*

E 2

force judg-
ment,
taking se-
curity, or
suspend
execution
pending
appeal.

the judgment or determination appealed against to be enforced, taking sufficient security for the performance of such order or decree as Her Majesty in Council may make on the appeal; or it may direct, on similar security being found, that no order for enforcing the judgment or determination shall be issued pending the appeal, and that, if any such order has been issued, it shall, so far as it has not been executed, be suspended.

Appellant
to find se-
curity for
costs of
appeal.

V. In either of the cases mentioned in the last preceding section, the Court shall require the appellant to find security for the payment of such costs as it may think likely to be incurred by the appeal.

Time al-
lowed for
presenting
petition of
appeal.

VI. If a party who is desirous of preferring an appeal to Her Majesty in Council, in any of the cases mentioned in Section I. or Section II. of this Act, shall require the assistance of the said Court for obtaining security from the other party for staying execution of the judgment, decree, or order that has been passed, or for any other purpose, he shall present his petition to the said Court within six calendar months from the date of the judgment, decree, or order appealed against.

If security
be found in-
adequate,
Court may
require it to
be increased

VII. If at any time pending an appeal under this act, the security taken from either party appears inadequate, whether from the increase or improvement of the property forming the subject of appeal, or from the insufficiency of the securities, the Court before which the appeal is pending may, on the application of the other party, require further security.

VIII. **In default of** such further security being found, if **the** original security was furnished by the appellant, the Court **may issue an** order for enforcing the judgment or determination appealed against as if no such original security **had been** given; and if the original security was furnished **by** the respondent, the Court, so far as may be practicable, shall compel him to deliver up the property forming the subject of appeal, which shall be disposed of in conformity with such of the rules in force as may be applicable to the particular case. *(If additional security be not furnished.)*

IX. In every case of appeal under this **Act, the** Court shall certify and transmit to Her Majesty **in** Council, under the seal of the Court, two true and correct copies of all evidence, proceedings, judgments, decrees, and orders had or made **in** the case appealed, so far as the same have relation to the matters of appeal, together with a copy of the **reasons** given by such Court for or against the judgment or determination appealed against. *(Proceedings in the suit appealed to be forwarded to Her Majesty in Council.)*

X. The **expense of preparing the** two aforesaid copies, and of translating into English so much of the original documents as may not **be in** that language, shall be defrayed by the **party** prosecuting the appeal. *(Expense of copying and translating papers in appeals to be paid by appellants.)*

XI. The Court shall cause the deposit by the appellant, within the time allowed for furnishing security for costs of appeal, **of** such a sum as shall be sufficient to cover the expense of making the two aforesaid copies; and when such deposit shall have been made, **and** not till then, shall declare the *(Court to require a deposit for such expense prior to the admission of an appeal.)*

appeal admitted, and give notice thereof to the appellant and respondent respectively.

Either party on paying for the same may obtain copy of any paper. XII. Either party, on application, may obtain one or more authenticated copies of any of the papers in the suit, on paying the reasonable expenses incurred in preparing them.

and of any local regulation or law. XIII. Either party, in like manner, may obtain an authenticated copy of any local regulation or law which he may require in the appeal.

Decrees of Her Majesty in Council, how to be obtained. XIV. The orders or decrees of Her Majesty in Council, when duly certified, shall be enforced and executed under the directions of the said Court by the judge or officer by whom the suit was originally tried, in the manner and according to the rules and laws applicable to the execution and enforcement of original orders or decrees made by such judge or officer.

Execution, how to be obtained. XV. Any party desirous of enforcing or obtaining execution of any such decree or order made in appeal as aforesaid, shall present a petition for that purpose to the Court which made the first decree or order appealed from, and the said petition shall be accompanied by a certified copy of the decree or order made in appeal and sought to be enforced or executed.

Appeal from order of enforcement. XVI. An appeal shall lie from any decree or order made by such last-mentioned Court relating to the enforcement or execution of any such decree or order made in appeal as aforesaid, in the same manner and subject to the same laws, rules, and regulations as an appeal from an order or decree made upon a petition for the enforcement of execution of the decree or order first appealed from would have been.

XVII. Nothing herein contained shall be construed so as to prevent the said Court of highest civil jurisdiction from enforcing or obtaining execution of a decree or order made or passed by Her Majesty in Council, if Her Majesty in Council shall think fit to decree or order the said Court to enforce or execute the same.

Court of highest civil jurisdiction may execute decrees by order of Her Majesty in Council.

XVIII. Nothing in this Act contained shall be understood to bar the full and unqualified exercise of Her Majesty's pleasure upon all appeals to her, either in rejecting any she may consider inadmissible, or in receiving any she may judge admissible.

Saving of Her Majesty's power as to receiving or rejecting appeals.

XIX. The words "British India" denote the territories which are or may become vested in Her Majesty by the statute 21 & 22 Vict. c. 106, entitled, "An Act for the better Government of India."

Interpretation of "British India."

AUSTRALIA.

NEW SOUTH WALES, VICTORIA, SOUTH AUSTRALIA, AND WESTERN AUSTRALIA.

The following Orders in Council have been printed respecting appeals from the three first named places. No order has been printed respecting Western Australia, nor does it appear that any has been issued.

NEW SOUTH WALES.

Order in Council making provision for Appeals from the Decisions of the Supreme Court of New South Wales.

AT THE COURT AT WINDSOR,

the 13th day of November, 1850.

PRESENT:

THE QUEEN'S MOST EXCELLENT MAJESTY IN COUNCIL.

WHEREAS by an Act passed in the Session of Parliament holden in the fourth and fifth years of his late Majesty King George the Fourth, entitled "An Act to provide until the 1st day of July, 1827, and until the end of the next Session of Parliament, for the better administration of justice in New South Wales and Van Diemen's Land, and for the more effectual government thereof, and for other purposes relating thereto," which Act was continued until the 31st of December, 1829, by an Act passed in

7 & 8 Geo. 4, c 37.

the Session of Parliament held in the 7th and 8th years of his said Majesty's reign, it was, amongst other things, provided, that it should be lawful for his then Majesty, his heirs and successors, by Charters and Letters Patent under the Great Seal of the United Kingdom of Great Britain and Ireland, to erect and establish a Court of Judicature in New South Wales, which should be styled "The Supreme Court of New South Wales," subject to the further regulations and provisions of the said Act.   And whereas, in pursuance of the authority

vested in him by the said first recited Act, his late
Majesty King George the Fourth did, by Letters
Patent bearing date the 13th day of October, 1824,
grant, direct, ordain, and appoint that there should
be within that part of the Colony of New South
Wales, situate in the Island of New Holland, a
Court which should be styled " The Supreme Court
of New South Wales ; " and did by the said Letters
Patent, in pursuance of such authority as aforesaid,
make further provisions respecting the powers and
jurisdiction of the said Court.

And whereas by another Act passed in the ninth 9 Geo. 4,
year of his said late Majesty, entitled " An Act to _{c. 83.}
provide for the Administration of Justice in New
South Wales and Van Diemen's Land, and for the
more effectual government thereof, and for other
purposes relating thereto," it was, amongst other
things, enacted that it should be lawful for His
Majesty, his heirs and successors, by Charters and
Letters Patent under the Great Seal of the United
Kingdom of Great Britain and Ireland, to erect and
establish a Court of Judicature in New South
Wales, which should be styled the Supreme Court
of New South Wales, subject to the further regulations in the said last-mentioned Act contained : and
it was thereby further enacted, that until His
Majesty should cause such Charters or Letters
Patent to be issued as aforesaid, the Supreme Court
of New South Wales, instituted by his said Majesty's
recited Letters Patent of the 13th day of October,
1824, should retain the several jurisdictions and
powers in the said Court vested by His Majesty's

last-mentioned Letters Patent (so far as the same might not be altered by the now reciting Act), as fully and as effectually as if such Court had been instituted in virtue and in pursuance of the said now reciting Act.

And whereas by the said last-mentioned Act it was further provided that it should be lawful for His Majesty, by the said Charters or Letters Patent respectively, or by any Order or Orders of His Majesty in Council, to allow any person or persons feeling aggrieved by any judgment, decree, order, or sentence of the said Supreme Courts respectively, to appeal therefrom to His Majesty in Council, in such manner, within such time, and under and subject to such rules, regulations, and limitations as His Majesty by any such Charters or Letters Patent, or Order or Orders in Council respectively, shall appoint and prescribe.

And whereas no such Charters or Letters Patent, or Orders in Council, have hitherto issued under the authority of the said last-mentioned Act ; and whereas it is expedient that provision should be made to enable parties to appeal from the decisions of the said Supreme Court to Her Majesty in Council. It is hereby ordered by the Queen's most Excellent Majesty, by and with the advice of Her Privy Council, that any person or persons may appeal to us, our heirs, and successors, in our or their Privy Council, from any final judgment, decree, order, or sentence of the said Supreme Court of New South Wales, in such manner, within such time, and under and subject to such rules, regulations, and limitations, as are hereinafter mentioned ; that is to say, in case any such judgment, decree, order, or sentence shall be given or pronounced **for** or in respect of any sum or matter at issue above the amount or value of 500*l.* sterling, or **in** case such judgment, decree, order, or sentence shall involve directly or indirectly any claim, demand, or question to or respecting property or any civil right amounting to or of the value of 500*l.* sterling, the person or persons feeling aggrieved by any such judgment, decree, order, or **sentence may, within** fourteen days next after the same shall have **been** pronounced, made, or given, **apply** to the **said** Court, by petition, for leave to appeal therefrom to us, our heirs, and successors, in our or their Privy Council ; and in case such leave to appeal shall be prayed by the party or parties who is or are directed to pay any such sum of money, or perform any **duty, the** said Court shall and is hereby empowered either to direct that the judgment, decree, order, or sentence appealed from shall be carried into execution, or that the execution thereof shall be suspended pending the said appeal, **as** to the said Court may appear to be most consistent with real and **sub**stantial justice ; and in case the said Court shall direct such judgment, decree, order, or sentence **to** be carried into execution, the person or **persons in** whose favour the same shall be given, shall before the execution thereof enter into good and sufficient security, to be approved **by** the said Court, for the due performance of such judgment or order, as we, our heirs, and successors shall think fit to make thereupon ; or in case the said Court shall direct the execution of any such judgment, decree, order, or sentence to be suspended pending the appeal, the person or persons against whom the same shall have been given, shall in like manner and before any order for the suspension of any such execution is made, enter into good and sufficient security to the said Court for the due performance of such judgment or order, as we, our heirs and successors, shall think fit to make thereupon, and in all cases we will and require that security shall also be given by the party or parties appellant, to the satisfaction of the said Court, for the prosecution of the appeal, and the payment of all such costs as may be awarded by us, our heirs, and successors, or by the Judicial Committee of our Privy Council, to the party respondent, and if such last-mentioned security shall be entered into within three months from the date of such petition for leave to appeal, then, and not otherwise, the said Court shall allow the appeal, and the party or parties appellant shall be at liberty to prefer and prosecute his, her, or their appeal to us, our heirs and successors, in our or their Privy Council, in such manner and under such rules as are or may be observed in appeals made to us from our plantations or colonies.

And further it is our will and pleasure, that it shall be lawful for the said Supreme Court of New South Wales, at its discretion, on the petition of any party who considers himself aggrieved by any preliminary or interlocutory judgment, decree, order, or sentence of the said Supreme Court, to grant permission to such party to appeal against the same, to us, our heirs and successors, in our or their Privy Council, subject to the same rules, regulations, and limitations as are herein expressed respecting appeals from final judgments, decrees, orders, and sentences.

Provided also, that if in any action, suit, or other proceeding, it shall so happen that no final judgment, decree, order, or sentence, can be duly given in consequence of a disagreement of opinion between the judges of the said Supreme Court, then and in such case the final judgment, decree, order, or sentence may be entered pro formâ, on the petition of any of the parties to the action, suit, or other proceedings, according to the opinion of the Chief Justice, or, in his absence, of the senior Puisne Judge of the said Supreme Court : provided that such judgment, decree, order, or sentence shall be deemed a judgment, decree, order, or sentence of the Court for the purpose of an appeal against the same, but not for any other purpose.

And we do hereby further reserve to ourself, our heirs and successors, in our or their Privy Council, full power and authority, upon the humble petition at any time of any person or persons aggrieved by any judgment or determination of the said Court, to admit his, her, or their appeal therefrom, upon such terms, and upon such securities, limitations, restrictions, and regulations, as we or they shall think fit, and to reverse, correct, or vary such judgment or determination as to us or them shall seem meet.

And it is our further will and pleasure, that in

all cases of appeal allowed by the said Court or by us, our heirs or successors, the said Court shall certify and transmit to us, our heirs and successors, in our or their Privy Council, a true and exact copy of all evidence, proceedings, judgments, decrees, and orders, had or made in such cases appealed, so far as the same have relation to the matters of appeal, such copies to be certified under the seal of the said Court ; and that the said Court shall also certify and transmit to us, our heirs and successors, in our or their Privy Council, a copy of the reasons given by the judges of such Court, or by any of such judges, for or against the judgment or determination appealed against, where such reasons shall have been given in writing ; and, where such reasons shall have been given orally, then a statement in writing of the reasons given by the judges of such Court, or by any of such judges for or against the judgment or determination appealed against.

And we do further direct and ordain, that the said Court shall in all cases of appeal to us, our heirs or successors, conform to, and execute, or cause to be executed, such judgments and orders as we shall think fit to make in the premises, in such manner as any original judgment, decree or decretal order, or other order or rule of the said Court of New South Wales, should or might have been executed.

And the Right Honourable Earl Grey, one of Her Majesty's Principal Secretaries of State, is to give the necessary directions herein accordingly.

Wm. L. Bathurst.

VICTORIA.

Order in Council, making provision for Appeals from the Supreme Court of the Colony of Victoria to Her Majesty in Council.

AT THE COURT AT BUCKINGHAM PALACE,

the 9th day of June, 1860.

PRESENT :

THE QUEEN'S MOST EXCELLENT MAJESTY IN COUNCIL.

WHEREAS by an Act passed by the Governor and Legislative Council of the Colony of Victoria in the fifteenth year of Her Majesty's reign it was enacted, that there should be in the said colony a Court styled the "Supreme Court of the Colony of Victoria," with the power and jurisdiction therein mentioned; and that persons aggrieved by the decision of the said Court might, in certain cases therein mentioned, appeal therefrom to Her Majesty in Council, but that nothing contained in the said Act should be construed to affect the Royal Prerogative, or to abridge the power of Her Majesty to allow any person so aggrieved to appeal to Her Majesty at any time in such manner as Her Majesty would be graciously pleased to allow : And whereas by an Act passed in a session of Parliament holden in the seventh and eighth years of Her Majesty it was enacted, that it should be competent to Her Majesty, by any Order or Orders in Council, to provide for the admission of appeals to Her Majesty in

Council from any judgments, sentences, decrees, or orders of any Court of Justice within any British colony or possession abroad, although such court should not be a Court of Errors or Appeal within such colony or possession, and to make provision for the instituting and prosecuting such appeals, and for carrying into effect any such decisions or sentences as Her Majesty in Council should pronounce thereon : And whereas it is desirable that provision should be made to enable parties to appeal from the decisions of the said Supreme Court to Her Majesty in Council :

It is hereby ordered by the Queen's most excellent Majesty, by and with the advice of Her Privy Council, that any person or persons may appeal to Her Majesty, her heirs and successors, in her or their Privy Council, from any final judgment, decree, order, or sentence of the said Supreme Court of the Colony of Victoria, in such manner, within such time, and under and subject to such rules, regulations, and limitations as are hereinafter mentioned ; that is to say, in case any such judgment, decree, order, or sentence shall be given or pronounced for or in respect of any sum or matter at issue above the amount or value of five hundred pounds sterling (500*l*.), or in case such judgment, decree, order, or sentence shall involve, directly or indirectly, any claim, demand, or question to or respecting property, or any civil right amounting to or of the value of five hundred pounds sterling (500*l*.), the person or persons feeling aggrieved by any such judgment, decree, order, or sentence may,

within fourteen days next after the same shall have
been pronounced, made, or given, apply to the said
Court, by motion or petition, for leave to appeal
therefrom to Her Majesty, her heirs and successors,
in her or their Privy Council; and in case such
leave to appeal shall be prayed by the party or
parties who is or are directed to pay any such sum
of money or perform any duty, the said Court shall
be and is hereby empowered, either to direct that
the judgment, decree, order, or sentence appealed
from shall be carried into execution, or that the
execution thereof shall be suspended pending the
said appeal, as to the said Court may appear to be
most consistent with real and substantial justice;
and in case the said Court shall direct such judgment, decree, order, or sentence to be carried into
execution, the person or persons in whose favour
the same shall be given shall, before the execution
thereof, enter into good and sufficient security, to be
approved by the said Court, for the due performance
of such judgment or order as Her Majesty, her heirs
and successors, shall think fit to make thereupon;
and in all cases security shall also be given by the
party or parties appellant in a bond or mortgage or
personal recognisance not exceeding the value of
500l. sterling for the prosecution of the appeal, and
the payment of all such costs as may be awarded by
Her Majesty, her heirs and successors, or by the
Judicial Committee of Her Majesty's Privy Council,
to the party or parties respondent; and if such last-
mentioned security shall be entered into within three
months from the date of such motion or petition for

leave to appeal, then, and not otherwise, the said Court shall allow the appeal, and the party or parties appellant shall be at liberty to prefer and prosecute his, her, or their appeal to Her Majesty, her heirs and successors, in her or their Privy Council, in such manner and under such rules as are or may be observed in appeals made to Her Majesty from Her Majesty's colonies and plantations abroad.

And it is further ordered, that it shall be lawful for the said Supreme Court, at its discretion, on the petition of any party who considers himself aggrieved by any preliminary or interlocutory judgment, decree, order, or sentence of the said Supreme Court, to grant permission to such party to appeal against the same to Her Majesty, her heirs and successors, in her or their Privy Council, subject to the same rules, regulations, and limitations as are herein expressed respecting appeals from final judgments, decrees, orders, and sentences.

Provided also, that if in any action, suit, or other proceeding it shall so happen that no final judgment, decree, order, or sentence can be duly given in consequence of a disagreement of opinion between the judges of the said Supreme Court, then and in such case the final judgment, decree, order, or sentence may be entered pro formâ, on the petition of any of the parties to the action, suit, or other proceedings, according to the opinion of the Chief Justice, or in his absence of the senior Puisne Judge of the said Supreme Court, provided that such judgment, decree, order, or sentence shall be deemed a judgment, decree, order, or sentence of the Court for the purpose of an appeal **against the same, but not for any other** purpose.

Provided always, and it is hereby ordered, that **nothing herein** contained doth **or shall extend** or be construed to extend to take away or abridge **the un-**doubted right and authority of Her Majesty, her heirs and successors, upon the humble petition **at** any time of **any person or** persons aggrieved by any judgment or determination of the said **Court, to** admit his, her, or their appeal therefrom, upon such terms, and upon **such securities, limitations, restric-**tions, and regulations, as Her Majesty, **her heirs or** successors, **shall think** fit, and to **reverse, correct, or** vary such judgment or determination **as to Her** Majesty, her heirs and successors, shall **seem meet.**

And it **is** further ordered, that in **all** cases of appeal allowed **by the** said Court, or by **Her Ma-**jesty, her heirs or successors, the said Court shall certify and transmit to Her Majesty, her heirs and successors, in her or their Privy Council, a true and exact copy of all evidence, proceedings, judgments, decrees, and orders had or made in such cases appealed, so far as the same have relation to the matters of appeal, such copies to be certified under the seal of the said Court; and that the said Court shall also certify and transmit to Her Majesty, her heirs and successors, in her or their Privy Council, a copy of the reasons given by the judges of such Court, or by any of such judges, for or against the judgment or determination appealed against, where such reasons shall have been given in writing, and where such **reasons shall have** been given orally then a statement in writing of the reasons given by the judges of such Court, or by any of such judges, for or against the judgment or determination appealed against.

And it is further directed and ordained, that the said Court shall, in all cases of appeal to Her Majesty, her heirs or successors, conform to and execute, or cause to be executed, such judgments and orders as Her Majesty, her heirs and successors, shall think fit to make in the premises, in such manner as any original judgment, decree, or decretal order, or other order or rule of the said Court, should or might have been executed.

And the Most Noble the Duke of Newcastle, one of Her Majesty's Principal Secretaries of State, is to give the necessary directions herein accordingly.

ARTHUR HELPS.

SOUTH AUSTRALIA.

Order in Council making provision for Appeals from the Supreme Court of the Province of South Australia to Her Majesty in Council.

AT THE COURT AT BUCKINGHAM PALACE,

the 9th day of June, 1860.

PRESENT :

THE QUEEN'S MOST EXCELLENT MAJESTY IN COUNCIL.

WHEREAS by an Act passed by the Governor and Legislative Council of the colony of South Australia, in the seventh year of the reign of His late Majesty William IV., it was enacted, that there should be in the said colony a Court styled " The Supreme Court of the Province of South Australia," with the power and jurisdiction therein mentioned, and that, subject to the rules therein mentioned, persons might appeal to Her Majesty in Council from the decisions of the said Court, in such manner and under such rules as are observed in appeals made to Her Majesty from Her Majesty's other plantations and colonies : And whereas by an Act passed in a session of Parliament holden in the seventh and eighth years of Her Majesty it was enacted, that it should be competent to Her Majesty, by any Order or Orders in Council, to provide for the admission of appeals to Her Majesty in Council from any judgments, sentences, decrees, or orders of any Court of Justice within any British colony or possession abroad, although such Court should not be a Court of Errors or Appeal within such colony or possession, and to make provision for the instituting and prosecuting such appeals, and for carrying into effect any such decisions or sentences as Her Majesty in Council shall pronounce thereon : And whereas it is desirable that provision should be made to enable parties to appeal from the decisions of the said Supreme Court to Her Majesty in Council :

It is hereby ordered by the Queen's most excellent Majesty, by and with the advice of Her Privy Council, that any person or persons may appeal to Her Majesty, her heirs and successors, in her or their Privy Council, from any final judgment, decree,

7 & 8 Vict. c. 69.

order, or sentence of the said Supreme Court of the Province of South Australia, in such manner, within such time, and under and subject to such rules, regulations, and limitations as are hereinafter mentioned; that is to say, in case any such judgment, decree, order, or sentence shall be given or pronounced for or in respect of any sum or matter at issue above the amount or value of five hundred pounds sterling (500*l.*), or in case such judgment, decree, order, or sentence shall involve, directly or indirectly, any claim, demand, or question to or respecting property, or any civil right amounting to or of the value of five hundred pounds sterling (500*l.*), the person or persons feeling aggrieved by any such judgment, decree, order, or sentence may, within fourteen days next after the same shall have been pronounced, made, or given, apply to the said Court, by motion or petition, for leave to appeal therefrom to Her Majesty, her heirs and successors, in her or their Privy Council; and in case such leave to appeal shall be prayed by the party or parties who is or are directed to pay any such sum of money or perform any duty, the said Court shall be and is hereby empowered, either to direct that the judgment, decree, order, or sentence appealed from shall be carried into execution, or that the execution thereof shall be suspended pending the said appeal, as to the said Court may appear to be most consistent with real and substantial justice; and in case the said Court shall direct such judgment, decree, order, or sentence to be carried into execution, the person or persons in whose favour

the same shall be given shall, before the execution
thereof, enter into good and sufficient security, to
be approved by the said Court, for the due performance of such judgment or order as Her Majesty, her
heirs and successors, shall think fit to make thereupon; and in all cases security shall also be given
by the party or parties appellant in a bond, or
mortgage, or personal recognisance, not exceeding
the value of five hundred pounds sterling (500*l.*),
for the prosecution of the appeal, and the payment
of all such costs as may be awarded by Her Majesty,
her heirs and successors, or by the Judicial Committee of Her Majesty's Privy Council, to the party
or parties respondent; and if such last-mentioned
security shall be entered into within three months
from the date of such motion or petition for leave
to appeal, then, and not otherwise, the said Court
shall allow the appeal, and the party or parties
appellant shall be at liberty to prefer and prosecute
his, her, or their appeal to Her Majesty, her heirs
and successors, in her or their Privy Council, in
such manner and under such rules as are or may
be observed in appeals made to Her Majesty from
Her Majesty's colonies and plantations abroad.

And it is further ordered, that it shall be lawful
for the said Supreme Court, at its discretion, on
the petition of any party who considers himself
aggrieved by any preliminary or interlocutory judgment, decree, order, or sentence of the said Supreme
Court, to grant permission to such party to appeal
against the same to Her Majesty, her heirs and
successors, in her or their Privy Council, subject to

the same rules, regulations, and limitations as are herein expressed respecting appeals from final judgments, decrees, orders, and sentences.

Provided also, that if in any action, suit, or other proceeding it shall so happen that no final judgment, decree, order, or sentence can be duly given, in consequence of a disagreement of opinion between the judges of the said Supreme Court, then and in such case the final judgment, decree, order, or sentence may be entered pro formâ, on the petition of any of the parties to the action, suit, or other proceedings, according to the opinion of the Chief Justice, or in his absence of the senior Puisne Judge of the said Supreme Court; provided that such judgment, decree, order, or sentence shall be deemed a judgment, decree, order, or sentence of the Court for the purpose of an appeal against the same, but not for any other purpose.

Provided always, and it is hereby ordered, that nothing herein contained doth or shall extend or be construed to extend to take away or abridge the undoubted right and authority of Her Majesty, her heirs and successors, upon the humble petition at any time of any person or persons aggrieved by any judgment or determination of the said Court, to admit his, her, or their appeal therefrom, upon such terms, and upon such securities, limitations, restrictions, and regulations, as Her Majesty, her heirs or successors, shall think fit, and to reverse, correct, or vary such judgment or determination, as to Her Majesty, her heirs and successors, shall seem meet.

And it is further ordered, that in all cases of appeal allowed by the said Court, or by Her Majesty, her heirs or successors, the said Court shall certify and transmit to Her Majesty, her heirs or successors, in her or their Privy Council, a true and exact copy of all evidence, proceedings, judgments, decrees, and orders had or made in such cases appealed, so far as the same have relation to the matters of appeal, such copies to be certified under the seal of the said Court; and that the said Court shall also certify and transmit to Her Majesty, her heirs and successors, in her or their Privy Council, a copy of the reasons given by the judges of such Court, or by any of such judges for or against the judgment or determination appealed against, where such reasons shall have been given in writing, and where such reasons shall have been given orally then a statement in writing of the reasons given by the judges of such Court, or by any of such judges, for or against the judgment or determination appealed against.

And it is further directed and ordained, that the said Court shall, in all cases of appeal to Her Majesty, her heirs or successors, conform to and execute or cause to be executed such judgments and orders as Her Majesty, her heirs and successors, shall think fit to make in the premises, in such manner as any original judgment, decree, or decretal order, or other order or rule of the said Court, should or might have been executed.

And the Most Noble the Duke of Newcastle, one of Her Majesty's Principal Secretaries of

F

State, is to give the necessary directions herein accordingly.

ARTHUR HELPS.

CANADA.

Appeals to the Privy Council from Upper Canada are regulated by the following sections of the Consolidated Statutes of Upper Canada, chapter 13, page 72:—

Appeal final in matters not exceeding 4,000 dollars.
57. The judgment of the Court of Error and Appeal shall be final where the matter in controversy does not exceed the sum or value of four thousand dollars. (12 Vict. c. 63, s. 46.)

When appeal may be to the Queen in Privy Council.
58. In a case exceeding that amount, as well as in a case where the matter in question relates to the taking of any annual or other rent, customary or other duty or fee, or any like demand of a general and public nature affecting future rights, of what value or amount soever the same may be, an appeal shall lie to Her Majesty in her Privy Council. (12 Vict. c. 63, s. 46.)

Security to be given.
59. But no such appeal shall be allowed until the appellant has given security in two thousand dollars, to the satisfaction of the Court appealed from, that he will effectually prosecute the appeal and pay such costs and damages as may be awarded in case the judgment or decree appealed from be affirmed.   (12 Vict. c. 63, s. 46.)

60. Upon the perfecting of such security execu- **The execu-tion to be stayed.** tion shall be stayed in the original cause. (12 Vict. c. 63, s. 46 ; and see ante, ss. 16, 17, 35.)

61. But the provisions of the 16th section of this **The 16th section to apply.** Act shall apply to such appeal, and the completion of the security hereby required shall not have the effect of staying execution in the cause in the different cases to which the said section relates unless the provisions in the said section be complied with. (12 Vict. c. 63, s. 46.)

62. Every judge of the Court of Error and **The judges may approve of the sure-ties.** Appeal shall have authority to approve of and allow the security to be given by a party who intends to appeal to Her Majesty in her Privy Council, whether the application for such allowance be made during the sitting of the said Court or at any other time. (20 Vict. c. 5, s. 36.)

63. Costs awarded by Her Majesty in her Privy **Costs in final appeal.** Council upon an appeal shall be recoverable by the same process as costs awarded by the Court of Error and Appeal. (20 Vict. c. 5, s. 37.)

General Rules.

64. The judges of the Court of Error and Appeal, **The judges of Court of Appeal may make rules.** or any five or more of them, of whom the Chief Justice of Upper Canada and the Chancellor shall be two, may from time to time make such general rules and orders for the effectual execution of this Act, and of the intention and object hereof, and for fixing the costs to be allowed in respect of pro-ceedings in the Court, and for regulating the different proceedings in appeal, as to them may

seem expedient, and may also from time to time alter and amend any of the existing rules, or any rules made under the authority of this Act, and make other rules instead thereof; and until such rules be made, the present rules and the existing practice and mode of proceeding in the Court shall continue in force.   (20 Vict. c. 5, s. 38.)

The following are copies of the other sections referred to :—

Stay of Execution.

When perfected execution to be stayed.

16. Upon the perfecting of such security, execution shall be stayed in the original cause, except in the following cases.   (12 Vict. c. 63, s. 40.)

Exceptions.

Subject to certain exceptions, in which partial performance is required by delivery into Court.

1. If the judgment or decree appealed from directs the assignment or delivery of documents or personal property, the execution of the judgment or decree shall not be stayed until the things directed to be assigned or delivered have been brought into Court, or placed in the custody of such officer or receiver as the Court appoints, nor until security has been given to the satisfaction of the Court appealed from, and in such sum as that Court directs, that the appellant will obey the order of the Appellate Court.   (12 Vict. c. 63, s. 40, No. 2.)

Or by executing the instrument.

2. If the judgment or decree appealed from directs the execution of a conveyance or any other

instrument, the execution of the judgment or decree shall not be stayed until the instrument has been executed and deposited with the proper officer of the Court appealed from, to abide the judgment of the Appellate Court. (12 Vict. **c. 63, s. 40, No. 3.**)

3. **If the judgment** or decree appealed **from** directs **the sale or** delivery of possession of real **property or chattels** real, the execution of the judg- **ment or decree shall not be** stayed until security **has** been **entered** into to the satisfaction of the **Court** appealed **from, and in such** sum as **that** Court directs, that, during the possession **of the** property by the appellant, he will not **commit or** suffer to be committed any waste **on the property;** and that, if the judgment be affirmed, he **will** pay the value of the use and occupation **of the property** from the time **of** the appeal until the delivery of possession thereof; and **also,** in case the judgment **or decree is** for the sale of property and the payment **of** a deficiency arising upon the sale, that the appel- lant will pay **the deficiency.** (12 Vict. **c.** 63, s. 40, Nos. 4 **and 5.**)

Or by the giving of special se- curity not to commit waste.

4. If the judgment, order, or decree appealed from directs the payment of money, the execution **of** the judgment **or** decree shall not be stayed until **the** ap- pellant has given security, to the satisfaction of the Court appealed from, that if the judgment, order, or **decree,** or any part thereof, **be** affirmed, the appel- lant will pay the amount thereby directed to be paid, or the part thereof **as to** which the judgment may be affirmed **if it** be affirmed only as to part,

Or to pay debt and costs.

and all damages awarded against the appellant on the appeal.   (12 Vict. c. 63, s. 40, No. 1.)

When given, a fiat to stay execution to be granted.

17. When the security has been perfected and allowed, any judge of the Court appealed from may issue his fiat to the sheriff to whom any execution on the judgment or decree has issued to stay the execution, and the execution shall be thereby stayed, whether a levy has been made under it or not.   (18 Vict. c. 123, s. 1.)

Allowance of security to be a supersedeas of execution.

35. Proceedings in an appeal from a decision in a court of law shall be deemed a supersedeas of execution from the time of the allowance of the security, but if the grounds of error or appeal appear to be frivolous, the Court whose judgment is appealed from, or a judge upon summons, may order execution to issue, or to be proceeded with. (20 Vict. c. 5, s. 22.)

LOWER CANADA.

Appeals to the Privy Council from Lower Canada are regulated by the following sections of the Consolidated Statutes for Lower Canada, p. 657:—

Of Appeals to Her Majesty in her Privy Council.

In what cases an appeal lies

52. The judgment of the Court of Queen's Bench shall be final in all cases where the matter in dis-

pute does not exceed the sum or value of five hundred pounds sterling; but in cases exceeding that sum or value, as well as in all cases where the matter in question relates to any fee of office, duty, rent, revenue, or any sum of money payable to Her Majesty, or to any title to lands or tenements, annual rents, or such like matters or things, where the rights in future might be bound, an appeal shall lie to Her Majesty in her Privy Council, in that part of the United Kingdom of Great Britain and Ireland called England, though the immediate sum or value appealed for be less than five hundred pounds sterling, provided security be first duly given by the appellant that he will effectually prosecute his appeal and answer the condemnation, and also pay the costs and damages to be awarded by Her Majesty in her Privy Council, in case the judgment of the said Court is affirmed,—or provided that the appellant agrees and declares in writing, at the clerk's office of the Court appealed from, that he does not object to the judgment given against him being carried into effect according to law, on which condition he shall give sureties for the costs of appeal only, in case the appeal is dismissed, and on condition also that the appellee shall not be obliged to render and return to the appellant more than the net proceeds of the execution, with legal interest on the sum recovered, or the restitution of the real property, and of the net value of the produce and revenues of the real property whereof the respondent has been put in possession, by virtue of the execution, to be computed from the day he recovered

from the judgment of the Court of Queen's Bench to Her Majesty in her Privy Council.

the sum or possessed the real property until perfect restitution is made, but without any damage against the respondent, by reason of such execution, in case the judgment is reversed.   (34 Geo. 3, c. 6, s. 30 ; and 12 Vict. c. 37, s. 19.)

In such cases execution to be suspended, and for what time.

53. In all cases where an appeal is allowed to Her Majesty in her Privy Council, execution shall be suspended for six months from the day on which such appeal is allowed and from the expiration of that period to the final determination of the said appeal, if before the expiration of the said six months a certificate is filed in the Court having jurisdiction in appeal in Lower Canada, signed by the clerk of Her Majesty's Privy Council or his deputy, or any other person duly authorised by him, that such appeal has been lodged, and that proceedings have been had thereon before Her Majesty in her Privy Council ; but if no such certi-

Certificate of such appeal must be lodged to suspend execution beyond that period.

ficate is produced and filed in the Court having jurisdiction in appeal in Lower Canada within the said six months, the said appeal shall no longer operate as a stay of judgment and execution, but the party who obtained judgment in the said Court having jurisdiction in appeal may sue out execution as if no such appeal had been made or allowed. (20 Vict. c. 44, s. 19, superseding 34 G. 3. c. 6, s. 31.)

Duty of clerk of appeals as regards judgments rendered by Her Majesty in her Privy Council.

54. On any appeal to Her Majesty in her Privy Council from any judgment heretofore rendered by the former Court of Appeals for Lower Canada, or from any judgment rendered by the present Court of Queen's Bench, on the appeal side thereof, the

Clerk of Appeals shall register an official exemplification of the judgment of Her Majesty in her Privy Council immediately on the production of the same by any party interested therein, and without requiring a previous order of the Court or of any judge thereof for such registration ; and the said Clerk of Appeals shall also, with a copy of such exemplification and without requiring any such previous order, remit the record of the cause to the Court below, unless the judgment of Her Majesty in her Privy Council require some further proceeding to be had in the said Court of Queen's Bench ; provided that nothing contained in this *Proviso.* section shall extend to or affect any judgment rendered by Her Majesty in her Privy Council before the 30th day of August, 1851. (14 & 15 Vict. c. 88, s. 8.)

Of the limitation of the time for bringing certain Appeals.

55. In all cases where an appeal is by law *No appeal may be* allowed from the superior Court to the Court of *brought* Queen's Bench, as also where an appeal is by law *after one year from* allowed from the said Court of Queen's Bench to *rendering of* Her Majesty in her Privy Council, no appeal shall *judgment except in* be granted or allowed after the expiration of one *certain cases.* year from the date of the final judgment of the said Courts respectively, saving always and excepting every such judgment whereby the rights of persons under age, *femes covert*, or persons *non compos mentis*, or otherwise *interdits*, are bound, who may appeal

F 3

from any such judgment within one year after the disability under which they have respectively so laboured has ceased, and in case of the death of any person labouring under any of the said disabilities, his heir or heirs, if present in Lower Canada, may appeal from such judgment within one year after such death, or, if absent therefrom, within five

Case of judgment given against absentees. years ; and also, saving and excepting every such judgment given against any person absent from Lower Canada (who may appeal from any such judgment within five years from the date thereof, if he does not sooner return to Lower Canada), in which case no appeal shall be admitted after the expiration of one year from the date of such return ;

Case of death within a year of the person against whom the judgment was rendered. and in case of the death of any person within one year after any judgment given against him, his heir or heirs, if present in Lower Canada, may appeal from such judgment at any time before the expiration of a year from the death of such person, and, if absent, before the expiration of five years from the date of such judgment. (34 G. 3, c. 6, s. 32. See 12 Vict. c. 38, s. 37 ; 20 Vict. c. 44, s. 60.)

HOW THE APPEALABLE AMOUNT IS ESTIMATED.

Maharajah Suteeschunder Roy	*Appellant,*
and	
Guneschunder and others	*Respondents.*

Ranee Surnomoye	*Appellant,*
and	
Maharajah Suteeschunder Roy	*Respondent.*

Gooroopersar Khoond	*Appellant,*
and	
Juggutchunder and others	*Respondents.*

In these cases counsel applied for leave to appeal, when the following judgment was delivered by Mr. Justice Turner :—

"The question in each of these cases is, whether leave should be given to appeal to her Majesty in Council. In none of the cases has there been any application to the Sudder Court for leave to appeal.

"The reason of there having been no application to the Sudder Court, in two at least of the cases, for leave to appeal, is stated to have been that the Sudder Court has proceeded upon a certain rule as to cases in which there should be leave given to appeal, and that, according to the rules on which they have proceeded, leave would not have been given in those two particular cases.

" It is not very clear to their lordships on what particular grounds the Sudder Court has proceeded with reference to giving or refusing leave to appeal, but their lordships feel no doubt upon what grounds the Sudder Court ought to proceed in those cases.

" It is quite clear, in their lordships' judgment, that the matter must be regulated by the Order in Council of the 10th April, 1838 (a), and by that order the Sudder Courts are not to give leave to appeal unless the petition be presented within the limited time in the order, and unless the value of the matter in dispute in such appeal shall amount to the sum of 10,000 rupees at least, importing that the leave to appeal is to be given in cases where the value of the matter in dispute in the appeal does amount to the sum of 10,000 rupees. Now, where the appeal is from the whole decree, and if the decree has given an amount exceeding 10,000 rupees, it is clear that the matter which is in dispute in the appeal must exceed the sum of 10,000 rupees, for the question to be tried upon the appeal is whether the decree is or is not right ; that is to say, whether the decree has or has not properly ordered payment of a sum exceeding 10,000 rupees. Where, therefore, at the date of the judgment the sum which is recoverable under the decree of the Sudder Court is an amount exceeding 10,000 rupees, there, in their lordships' judgment, the case must clearly fall within the terms of the Order in Council.

(a) Now regulated by letters patent of 14th May, 1862.

" That, in their lordships' understanding, disposes of the first and third cases which are before us on the present occasion.

" The second case is somewhat different in its circumstances. That appears to be a case upon which the party applying for leave to appeal claims to be entitled to an estate subject only to the payment of sixty-four rupees. The plaintiff in the suit, who is in possession of the judgment of the Court below, and who would be the respondent upon the appeal, claims the right to set upon the estate any rent which he may think fit.

" The case appears to their lordships to admit of two considerations; whether, in the first place, the value in the appeal can be considered to be 10,000 rupees within the meaning of the order; but if it be not, then it is clearly a case which would be within the discretion of their lordships as to whether leave to appeal should or should not be given.

" Taking the case to be within the meaning of the order, it is clear that the value of the matter in dispute will exceed the sum of 10,000 rupees.

" Of course an estate held at a rent of sixty-four rupees must be diminished in value to a very considerable amount, far exceeding 10,000 rupees, if it be chargeable with a rent of 822 rupees, the amount of rent given by the decree. Their lordships therefore think, in that second case, viewing it as either falling within the order or within the discretion of the Court, the leave to appeal ought to be given.

" In all these cases their lordships have fully and at length entered into them, because they consider it of importance that the Sudder Court should perfectly understand the rule which ought to be proceeded on in giving leave to appeal. We therefore desire to lay down the rules I have mentioned upon the subject, and are of opinion that in all of these cases leave should be given to appeal, and that in each case security should be given to the amount of 300*l*."

RECORD PRINTED IN ENGLAND (*a*).

Appellant's Costs in an Indian Appeal.

IN THE PRIVY COUNCIL.

Name of court.

On appeal from

BETWEEN

Appellant,

Full title.

and

Respondent.

Note.—This and the following precedents of bills of costs contain all the usual items allowed on a party and party taxation ; any other charges of a similar nature should be added.

(*a*) In cases in which the record is printed abroad, this bill would be altered by an allowance of £1 1*s.* for perusing each printed folio sheet, instead of 6*s.* 8*d.* for each brief sheet ; and charges for correcting proofs and examining printed transcript with original would be omitted.

The appellant's costs to be taxed, as between party and party, pursuant to an order of the Judicial Committee of the Privy Council, dated ——— day of ———.

HILARY TERM, 1866.

	£	s.	d.
Retainer fee	0	13	4
Attending to enter appearance . .	0	10	0
Paid thereon	0	10	0
Attending bespeaking official copy of record, and signing undertaking to pay costs of same	0	10	0
Having received notice from Privy Council office that copy was ready, attending obtaining same . .	0	10	0
Paid stationer's charges for same . .	15	0	0
Paid cab	0	2	6
Paid messenger	0	2	6
Perusing official copy proceedings, 1500 folios, equal to 300 brief sheets, at 6s. 8d. per each three sheets .	33	6	8
Instructions for petition of appeal . .	0	10	0
Drawing same, folios 20 . . .	2	0	0
Attending counsel therewith to settle .	0	10	0
Paid his fee and clerk (a) . .	5	15	6
Copy petition for respondent's agent .	0	10	0
Attending respondent's agent therewith	0	10	0
Attending at Council office lodging petition of appeal	0	10	0
Paid	1	1	0

(a) Clerk's fee, 10s. 6d.

	£	s.	d.
Instructions for and preparing retainer to senior counsel	0	13	4
Attending him therewith	0	10	0
Paid his fee and clerk	2	7	0
Instructions for and preparing retainer to junior counsel	0	13	4
Attending him therewith	0	10	0
Paid his fee and clerk	2	7	0
Attending at Privy Council office, when I found respondent had not appeared	0	10	0
Drawing scheme for printing, and fair copy, folios 20	1	10	0
Attending at Privy Council office returning official copy for printing	0	10	0
Paid for printing 25 folio sheets	50	0	0
Attending at Privy Council office, examining printed copy with original (all day) (a)	2	2	0
Like this day (b)	2	2	0
Like this day	2	2	0
Like this day	2	2	0
Like this day	2	2	0
Correcting proofs, 25 sheets, at 1 guinea per folio sheet (b)	26	5	0

(a) To examine twenty-four printed pages per diem is considered a fair average.

(b) The proofs are usually examined with the original record, and are afterwards corrected as they come from the printer's. Any necessary attendances at the Council office to obtain appointments, or correspondence with the respondent's solicitors, should be added to these charges.

EASTER TERM.

	£	s.	d.
Attending at Privy Council office obtaining 5 prints of record . . .	0	10	0
Cab hire	0	2	6
Attending at Privy Council office, searching if respondent had yet appeared, when I found he had not . .	0	10	0
Drawing petition for order, and summons to respondent to appear . .	0	10	0
Engrossing same	0	2	6
Attending at Privy Council office to lodge same	0	10	0
Paid fee	1	1	0
Paid for committee order . . .	1	12	6
Paid messengers	0	2	6
Two copies of summons for posting .	0	5	0
Attending at Royal Exchange posting up a copy of summons . . .	0	10	0
Like attendance at Lloyd's Coffee House	0	10	0
The two months named in this summons having expired, attending at Privy Council office to search if respondent had appeared, when I found he had not	0	10	0
Drawing petition for peremptory order for respondent to enter appearance within six weeks	0	10	0
Engrossing	0	2	6
Attending to lodge	0	10	0
Paid on lodging	1	1	0
Drawing affidavit in support (a) . .	0	10	0

(a) No instructions are allowed.

	£	s.	d.
Copy to swear	0	2	6
Copy summons, and order to annex	0	5	0
Attending before Registrar swearing to affidavit	0	10	0
Paid fee on lodging	1	1	0
Paid fee for committee order	1	12	6
Making two copies of order for posting	0	5	0
Attending at Royal Exchange posting one copy order	0	10	0
Like attendance at Lloyd's Coffee House	0	10	0
Attending at Privy Council office searching, when I found respondent had appeared	0	10	0

TRINITY TERM.

	£	s.	d.
Instructions for appellant's case	1	0	0
Drawing same, folios 100 (a)	10	0	0
Making two fair copies of petition of appeal for counsel, folios 20 each	1	0	0
Attending junior counsel with papers to settle case	0	10	0
Paid his fee and clerk (b)	33	1	6
Two fair copies of case as settled by junior counsel to settle in conference, folios 100 each	5	0	0
Attending senior counsel with papers	0	10	0
Paid his fee and clerk	33	1	6
Attending both counsel, arranging for consultation	1	0	0

(a) 2s. per folio for drawing; 6d. per folio for copying.
(b) Clerk's fee, 1s. in the £.

	£	s.	d.
Paid consultation fee to senior counsel and clerk (a)	5	15	6
Attending him	0	10	0
Paid consultation fee to junior counsel .	5	15	6
Attending him	0	10	0
Attending consultation when case settled	1	0	0
Fair copy case for printer . . .	2	10	0
Attending him and instructing him to strike off proof	0	10	0
Correcting proof, three sheets (b) . .	3	3	0
Attending printer, instructing him to strike off 100 copies . . .	0	10	0
Paid printer's bill	6	6	0
Attending lodging case	0	10	0
Paid fee	1	1	0

MICHAELMAS TERM.

	£	s.	d.
Attending at Privy Council office to search if the respondent had brought in his case, when I found he had not done so	0	10	0
Drawing petition for respondent to lodge his case within one month, and fair copy	0	10	0
Engrossing same	0	2	6
Attending at Council office lodging petition	0	10	0
Paid fee	1	1	0
Paid for committee order . . .	1	12	6

(a) Clerk's fee, 10s. 6d.

(b) The printed case usually contains from fifty to sixty lines each printed page.

	£	s.	d.
Paid messenger	0	2	6
Copy order for service on appellant's agents	0	2	6
Attending serving same	0	10	0
Sessions fee	3	3	0

HILARY TERM, 1867.

	£	s.	d.
Attending Privy Council office searching if respondent had lodged his case, when I found that he had not	0	10	0
Drawing petition for peremptory order for respondent to lodge case	0	10	0
Engrossing same	0	2	6
Attending to lodge same at Privy Council office	0	10	0
Paid on lodging	1	1	0
Drawing affidavit in support (a)	0	10	0
Copy to swear	0	2	6
Attending before Registrar swearing to affidavit, and lodging same	0	10	0
Paid fee on lodging affidavit	1	1	0
Paid fee for committee order	1	12	6
Copy for service on respondent's agent	0	2	6
Attending serving him	0	10	0

EASTER TERM.

	£	s.	d.
Attending at Privy Council office, when I found that respondent had not yet appeared	0	10	0
Drawing petition for order to set down the appeal for hearing *ex parte*	0	10	0

(a) No instructions allowed.

	£	s.	d.
Engrossing same	0	2	6
Attending at Privy Council office to lodge same	0	10	0
Paid	1	1	0
Drawing affidavit in support . . .	0	10	0
Copy to swear	0	2	6
Attending before Registrar swearing and lodging same	0	10	0
Paid fee on lodging	1	1	0

TRINITY TERM.

	£	s.	d.
Having received a notice from the respondent's agent, informing me that he had lodged his case, writing him making an appointment to attend here and exchange	0	5	0
Attending respondent's agent exchanging copies of respective cases . .	0	10	0
Perusing respondent's case, four folio sheets (a)	2	2	0
Attending binder with proceedings, and instructing him to bind thirteen copies	0	10	0
Paid him binding	3	3	0

MICHAELMAS TERM.

	£	s.	d.
Paid for first summons for hearing .	0	10	0
Paid messenger	0	2	6
Copy for each counsel	0	5	0

(a) Allowed at 10s. 6d. per sheet.

	£	s.	d.
Attending senior counsel with brief (a)	1	0	0
Paid his fee and clerk	66	3	0
Attending junior counsel with brief	1	1	0
Paid his fee and clerk (b)	55	2	6
Attending senior counsel fixing consult-ation	0	10	0
Paid his fee and clerk	5	15	6
Attending junior counsel fixing consult-ation	0	10	0
Paid his fee and clerk	5	15	6
Attending consultation	1	0	0
Attending Council chamber all day, appeal not called on	2	6	8
Like attendance this day	2	6	8
Paid for second summons for hearing	0	10	0
Paid messenger	0	2	6
Two copies for counsel	0	5	0
Attending hearing this day	3	6	8

HILARY TERM.

	£	s.	d.
Refresher to senior counsel and clerk	11	1	6
Attending marking	0	10	0
Refresher to junior counsel and clerk	11	1	6
Attending marking	0	10	0
Paid for third summons for hearing	0	10	0
Paid messenger therewith	0	2	6
Two copies for counsel	0	5	0
Attending hearing this day	3	6	8
Refresher to senior counsel and clerk	11	1	6

(a) No instructions for brief or observations are allowed as between party and party.

(b) Clerk's fee, 1s. in the £.

	£	s.	d.
Attending marking	0	10	0
Refresher to junior counsel and clerk .	11	1	6
Attending marking	0	10	0
Paid for fourth summons for hearing .	0	10	0
Paid messenger therewith . . .	0	2	6
Two copies for counsel	0	5	0
Attending hearing this day . .	3	6	8
Paid summons to hear judgment . .	0	10	0
Paid messenger	0	2	6
Two copies for counsel	0	5	0
Attending senior counsel, marking his fee to attend and hear judgment . .	0	10	0
Paid his fee and clerk	5	10	6
Attending junior counsel, marking his fee to attend and hear judgment .	0	10	0
Paid his fee and clerk	5	10	6
Attending at Council chamber to hear judgment when same given for appellant	1	6	8
Attending at Council office drawing up minutes for committee report . .	1	1	0
Paid for committee report . . .	1	10	0
Paid messenger	0	2	6
Attending at Privy Council office paying fees and taking receipt . . .	0	10	0
Attending obtaining order to tax . .	0	10	0
Paid for order to tax	1	12	6
Copy and service	0	15	0
Drawing bill of costs and copy, folios 30 (a)	2	0	0

(a) 1s. per folio for drawing; 6d. per folio for copying.

	£	s.	d.
Copy for respondent's solicitors . .	0	15	0
Attending them therewith and with copy bill	0	10	0
Attending taxing	2	2	0
Fee on taxing	3	3	0
Paid for final order	3	2	6
Writing colonial correspondent informing him result of appeal . . .	0	5	0
Paid shorthand writer for taking notes of judgment, and for transcript . .	2	2	0
Attending paying for same and taking receipt	0	10	0
Sessions fee	3	3	0
Paid colonial and other petty cash throughout	4	4	0

Appellant's Costs for special leave to Appeal.

IN THE PRIVY COUNCIL.

Name of court.

On appeal from

Name of court.

Date of decree.

In the matter of a decree of ——, dated ——, in a suit

BETWEEN

Full title.

Appellants,

and

Respondents.

HILARY TERM, 1869.

	£	s.	d.
Retainer fee	0	13	4
Perusing papers sent by you in support of petition for leave to appeal, folios 300 (a)	6	13	4
Instructions for petition of appeal . .	1	0	0
Making copies of all the papers for counsel, folios 300 (b) . . .	7	10	0
Drawing petition, folios 100 (c) . .	10	0	0
Attending counsel therewith to settle .	0	10	0
Paid his fee and clerk . . .	5	15	6
Fair copy petition as settled by counsel, folios 100	2	10	0
Engrossing same to present (d) . .	5	0	0
Attending lodging petition of appeal .	0	10	0
Paid on lodging	1	1	0
Instructions for and drawing affidavit in support of petition, and engrossing same	0	10	0
Attending to be sworn	0	10	0
Paid entering petition . . .	0	10	0
Attending lodging original papers in Council office	0	10	0
Instructions for and drawing brief in support of petition, and drawing observations and fair copy . .	2	2	0
Attending counsel therewith . . .	0	10	0

(a) 6s. 8d. for each 25 folios.
(b) 6d. per folio for copying.
(c) 2s. per folio for drawing.
(d) 1s. per folio.

G

	£	s.	d.
Paid his fee and clerk . . .	5	15	6
Attending setting down petition . .	0	10	0
Paid	0	10	0
Paid summons	0	10	0
Paid messenger therewith . . .	0	2	6
Attending Council chamber when peti-			
tion heard, order made . . .	1	6	8
Attending at Privy Council office draw-			
ing up minutes for committee report	1	1	0
Paid committee report	1	10	0
Paid messenger	0	2	6
Attending at Privy Council office paying			
fees and taking receipt . . .	0	10	0
Paid for final order	3	2	6
Writing colonial agent informing him			
of result of application . . .			
Paid shorthand writer . . .	2	2	0
Sessions fee (a)	3	3	0
Paid petty charges	1	1	0

Note.—When the appeal is admitted, these items for obtaining special leave to appeal will be allowed against the respondent in appeals in which the appellant succeeds.

(a) Not always allowed.

RECORD PRINTED IN ENGLAND (a).

Respondent's Costs in an Indian Appeal.

IN THE PRIVY COUNCIL.

On appeal from

BETWEEN

Name of court.

Appellant,

and

Full title.

Respondent.

The respondent's costs to be taxed, as between party and party, pursuant to an order of the Judicial Committee of the Privy Council, dated the —— day of ——, 186—.

HILARY TERM, 1867.

	£	s.	d.
Retainer fee	0	13	4
Attending to enter appearance . .	0	10	0
Paid thereon	0	10	0
Writing appellant's agent informing him I had entered an appearance . .	0	5	0

(a) In cases in which the record is printed abroad, this bill would be **altered by an** allowance **of** 1l. 1s. **for perusing** each printed **folio sheet** instead of 6s. 8d. for each brief sheet ; and **charge for** correcting proofs and examining printed transcript with original would be **omitted.**

	£	s.	d.
Attending appellant's agent on his calling, and arranging with him to go through copy record to settle what should be printed	0	10	0
Perusing official copy proceedings, 1000 folios, equal to 120 brief sheets, at 6s. 8d. for each three sheets	13	6	8
Perusing order for leave to appeal, folios 20	0	6	8
Attending returning official copy to appellant's agent, and arranging what parts should be printed	0	10	0

EASTER TERM.

	£	s.	d.
Instructions for and preparing retainer to leading counsel	0	13	4
Attending him therewith	0	10	0
Paid his fee and clerk	2	7	0
Instructions for and preparing retainer to junior counsel	0	13	4
Attending him therewith	0	10	0
Paid his fee and clerk	2	7	0
Attending all day at Privy Council office examining printed copy of transcript with original (a)	2	2	0

(a) To examine twenty-four printed pages per day is considered a fair average. The proofs are usually examined with original, and afterwards corrected as the sheets come from the printer. Any necessary correspondence with the appellant's agent respecting this examination should be charged for.

	£	s.	d.
Like attendance this day . . .	2	2	0
Like attendance this day . . .	2	2	0
Correcting proofs, 18 printed sheets .	18	18	0
Attending at the Privy Council office obtaining five printed copies of transcript and record	0	10	0
Cab hire	0	2	6
Instructions for case of respondent .	1	0	0
Drawing same, folios 80 (a) . . .	8	0	0
Making two fair copies petition of appeal for counsel, folios 20 each (b) . .	1	0	0
Attending junior counsel with papers to settle case	0	10	0
Paid his fee and clerk	22	1	0
Two fair copies of case as settled by junior counsel to settle in conference, folios 80 each	4	0	0
Attending senior counsel with papers .	0	10	0
Paid his fee and clerk . . .	22	1	0
Attending both counsel, arranging and fixing time for consultation . . .	1	0	0

TRINITY TERM.

	£	s.	d.
Paid consultation fee to senior counsel and clerk	5	15	6
Attending him therewith . . .	0	10	0
Paid consultation fee to junior counsel and clerk	5	15	6

(a) 2s. per folio for drawing case.
(b) 6d. per folio for copying.

	£	s.	d.
Attending him therewith . . .	0	10	0
Attending consultation when case settled	1	0	0
Fair copy of case for the printer, folios 80	2	0	0
Attending printer, instructing him to strike off proof (a) . . .	0	10	0
Correcting proof (two sheets) . . .	2	2	0
Attending printer therewith, instructing him to print 100 copies . . .	0	10	0
Paid printer's bill			
Attending at the Privy Council office lodging printed case . . .	0	10	0
Paid fee	1	1	0

MICHAELMAS TERM.

	£	s.	d.
Attending at Privy Council office to search if appellant had brought in his case, when I found he had not done so	0	10	0
Drawing petition for appellant to lodge his case within one month, and fair copy	0	10	0
Engrossing same	0	2	6
Attending at Council office lodging petition	0	10	0
Paid fee	1	1	0
Paid for committee order . . .	1	12	6
Paid messenger.	0	2	6
Copy of order for service on appellant's agents	0	2	6

(a) *Vide ante*, page 115.

	£	s.	d.
Attending serving same . . .	0	10	0
Attending **Privy** Council office searching if appellant had lodged his case, when I found that he had not . . .	0	10	0
Drawing petition for peremptory. order for appellant to lodge case . .	0	10	0
Engrossing same	0	2	6
Attending to lodge same at Privy Council Office	0	10	0
Paid on lodging	1	1	0
Drawing affidavit **in** support . .	0	10	0
Copy to swear	0	2	6
Attending before Registrar **swearing to affidavit** and lodging same . .	0	10	0
Paid fee on lodging affidavit . . .	1	1	0
Paid fee for committee order . .	1	12	6
Copy for service on appellant's **agents** .	0	2	6
Attending serving him . . .	0	10	0
Sessions **fee**	3	3	0

HILARY TERM.

	£	s.	d.
Attending at Privy Council office, **when** I found that appellant **had** not **yet** lodged his case	0	10	0
Drawing petition for order **to** set down the appeal for hearing *ex parte* . .	0	10	0
Engrossing same	0	2	6
Attending **at** Privy Council office to **lodge same**	0	10	0
Paid	1	1	0

	£	s.	d.
Drawing affidavit in support . . .	0	10	0
Copy to swear	0	2	6
Attending before Registrar swearing and lodging same	0	10	0
Paid fee on lodging	1	1	0
Having received a notice from the appellant's agent informing me that he had lodged his case, writing him making an appointment to attend here and exchange	0	5	0
Attending appellant's agent, exchanging copies of respective cases . .	0	10	0
Perusing appellant's case, 4 sheets (a) .	2	2	0
Attending binder with proceedings to bind (three copies)	0	10	0
Paid him binding			

Easter Term.

	£	s.	d.
Paid for first summons for hearing .	0	10	0
Paid messenger	0	2	6
Copy for each counsel . . .	0	5	0
Attending senior counsel with brief (b)	1	0	0
Paid his fee and clerk . . .	44	2	0
Attending junior counsel with brief . .	0	10	0
Paid his fee and clerk . . .	33	1	6
Attending senior counsel, fixing consultation	0	10	0

(a) Usually allowed at the rate of 10s. 6d. per sheet.

(b) When the fee is over 30 guineas, 1l. is allowed for this attendance ; if under 30 guineas, 10s. 6d. only.

	£	s.	d.
Paid his fee and clerk . . .	5	15	6
Attending junior counsel, fixing consultation	0	10	0
Paid his fee and clerk . . .	5	15	6
Attending Council Chamber all day, appeal not called on	2	6	8
Paid for second summons for hearing .	0	10	0
Paid messenger	0	2	6
Two copies for counsel	0	5	0
Attending hearing this day . . .	3	6	8

TRINITY TERM.

	£	s.	d.
Refresher to senior counsel and clerk .	11	1	6
Attending marking	0	10	0
Refresher to junior counsel and clerk .	11	1	6
Attending marking	0	10	0
Paid for third summons for hearing . .	0	10	0
Paid messenger therewith . . .	0	2	6
Two copies for counsel	0	5	0
Attending hearing this day . .	3	6	8
Paid summons to hear judgment . .	0	10	0
Paid messenger	0	2	6
Two copies for counsel	0	5	0
Attending senior counsel, marking his fee to attend and hear judgment .	0	10	0
Paid his fee and clerk	5	10	6
Attending junior counsel, marking his fee to attend and hear judgment . .	0	10	0
Paid his fee and clerk . . .	5	10	6
Attending at Council Chamber to hear judgment	1	6	8

	£	s.	d.
Attending at Council office, drawing up minutes for committee report	1	1	0
Paid for committee report	1	10	0
Paid messenger	0	2	6
Attending at Privy Council office, paying fees and taking receipt	0	10	0
Attending obtaining order to tax	0	10	0
Paid for order to tax	1	12	6
Copy and service	0	15	0
Drawing bill of costs and copy, folios 20 (a)	1	10	0
Copy for appellant's solicitors	0	10	0
Attending them therewith	0	10	0
Attending taxing	2	2	0
Fee on taxing	3	3	0
Paid for final order	3	2	6
Writing colonial correspondent informing him of result of appeal	0	5	0
Paid shorthand writer for taking notes of judgment, and for transcript			
Attending, paying for same and taking receipt	0	10	0
Sessions fee	3	3	0
Paid colonial and other petty cash throughout	4	4	0

(a) At rate of 1s. per folio for drawing.

RECORD PRINTED IN ENGLAND.

Respondent's Costs of Appeal from a Colonial Court.

IN THE PRIVY COUNCIL.

On appeal from the Supreme Court of the Colony of Victoria (in Equity).

BETWEEN

Appellants, **Full title.**

and

Respondents.

Costs of the Respondents.

To be taxed as between party and party, pursuant to an Order of the Judicial Committee of the Privy Council, dated ―――― day of ――――, 186―.

EASTER TERM, 1867.

	£	s.	d.
Retainer fee	0	13	4
Attending at the Council office, entering appearance	0	10	0
Paid appearance fee	0	10	0
Writing the appellant's agents, informing them I had entered an appearance	0	5	0
Perusing order for leave to appeal and copy petition of appeal . . .	1	1	0
Perusing official copy of the proceedings in the colony (99 brief sheets) . .	11	0	0

	£	s.	d.
Writing appellant's agents to know whether amount ordered to be deposited as security for costs had been deposited	0	5	0
Attending them on their bringing receipt for the 300*l.* deposit, and inspecting same	0	10	0
Attending appellant's agent on his calling, and going through copy record, and arranging with him what portions should be printed . .	0	10	0
Perusing official copy proceedings, 1500 folios, equal to 180 brief sheets, at 6s. 8d. for each three sheets . .	20	0	0
Perusing petition for leave to appeal .	1	1	0
Attending returning official copy to appellant's agent, and arranging what part should be printed . . .	0	10	0
Attending at Privy Council office, examining printed copy transcript with original (a)	2	2	0
Like attendance this day . . .	2	2	0
Like attendance this day . . .	2	2	0
Like attendance this day . . .	2	2	0
Like attendance this day . . .	2	2	0
Like attendance this day . . .	2	2	0
Attendances examining proof prints of record (25 folio sheets) . . .	13	2	6
Attending the Privy Council office for and obtaining printed copies of record	0	10	0

(a) *Vide* note (b), *ante,* p. 112.

	£	s.	d.
Cab hire	0	2	6
Instructions for and preparing retainer to senior counsel	0	13	4
Attending him therewith . .	0	10	0
Paid his fee and clerk . . .	2	7	0
Instructions for and preparing retainer to junior counsel	0	13	4
Attending him therewith . .	0	10	0
Paid his fee and clerk . . .	2	7	0
Attending Council office, and obtaining five copies of printed transcript . .	0	10	0
Paid cab	0	2	6

MICHAELMAS TERM, 1867.

	£	s.	d.
Instructions for respondent's case . .	1	0	0
Drawing same (folios 70) . . .	7	0	0
Making two fair copies of petition of appeal for counsel (folios 20 each) .	1	0	0
Attending junior counsel with papers to settle case	0	10	0
Paid his fee and clerk . . .	33	1	6
Two fair copies of case as settled by junior for final settlement in consultation (folios 100 each) . . .	5	0	0
Attending senior counsel with papers .	0	10	0
Paid his fee and clerk . . .	33	1	6
Attending both counsel fixing consultation	1	0	0
Paid consultation fee to senior counsel	5	15	6
Attending him	0	10	0
Paid consultation fee to junior counsel .	5	15	6

	£	s.	d.
Attending him	0	10	6
Fair copy respondent's case for printer (folios 100)	2	10	0
Attending printer, instructing him to print proofs	0	10	0
Correcting proofs (three printed sheets) .	1	11	6
Attending printer with corrected print, and instructing him to print 100 copies	0	10	0
Paid printer's charges	6	6	0
Attending to lodge respondent's case at Privy Council office . . .	0	10	0
Paid fee on lodging . . .	1	1	0
Cab hire	0	2	6
Writing the appellant's agents, making appointment to exchange cases . .	0	5	0
Attending them exchanging cases .	0	10	0
Perusing appellant's case (four sheets) .	2	2	0
Sessions fee	3	3	0

HILARY TERM, 1865.

	£	s.	d.
Attending at the Privy Council office to ascertain if the appeal was set down .	0	10	0
Paid fee for setting down . . .	0	10	0
Attending senior counsel with brief .	1	0	0
Paid his fee and clerk . . .	66	3	0
Attending junior counsel with brief .	1	0	0
Paid his fee and clerk	44	2	0
Attending senior counsel appointing consultation	0	10	0
Paid his fee and clerk	5	15	6

	£	s.	d.
Attending him	0	10	0
Attending junior counsel appointing consultation	0	10	0
Paid his fee and clerk . . .	5	15	6
Paid for first summons to attend hearing	0	10	0
Paid messenger therewith . . .	0	2	6
Two copies for counsel	0	5	0
Attending consultation . . .	1	0	0
Attending Council chamber all day ; appeal in the paper, but not heard . .	2	6	8
Paid for second summons for hearing .	0	10	0
Paid messenger therewith . . .	0	2	6
Two copies for counsel . . .	0	5	0
Attending Council chamber all day ; appeal again in the paper, but not heard	2	6	8
Paid for third summons to attend hearing	0	10	0
Paid messenger therewith . . .	0	2	6
Two copies for counsel . . .	0	5	0
Attending Council chamber all day ; appeal heard, and judgment given, dismissing same, with costs . . .	3	6	8
Attending at Council office on the drawing up of minutes for committee report	1	1	0
Paid for committee report . . .	1	10	0
Attending obtaining order to tax . .	0	10	0
Paid for order to tax costs . . .	1	12	6
Copy and service	0	15	0

	£	s.	d.
Drawing this bill of costs and copy folios (14)	1	1	0
Copy for appellant's agents . . .	0	7	0
Attending them therewith, and with appointment for taxation. . .	0	10	0
Attending taxation	2	2	0
Paid taxing fee	3	3	0
Paid order of Her Majesty in Council .	3	2	6
Writing colonial correspondent, with final order, and thereon . . .	0	5	0
Paid shorthand writer for taking notes of judgment, and for transcript thereof			
Attending paying same and taking receipt	0	10	0
Sessions fee	3	3	0
Paid colonial and other postage, and petty expenses throughout .	3	3	0

PETITION OF APPEAL.

In the Privy Council.

On appeal from the High Court of Judicature at Fort William, in Bengal.

Between

Appellant,   **Full title.**

and

Respondents.

To the Queen's Most Excellent Majesty in Council.

The humble petition of ——, the above-named appellant,

Sheweth,

That on the —— day of ——, 186—, your petitioner filed a plaint in the Court of the Principal Sudder Ameen of Zillah (——) against the above-named respondents and defendants, to recover possession, by right of inheritance, of the Zemindary Talooks and Mehals, permanently and summarily settled, mentioned in Schedule No. 1 annexed to the said plaint, left by —— Zemindar, deceased, paternal grandfather of the minors, viz., —— and ——, in Zillah (——), and Pergunnah (——) and (——), Pergunnah (——), comprised in the said Zillah (——) and Zillah (——), and the houses mentioned in Schedule No. 2 to the said plaint, also annexed, and for possession or the value of personal properties mentioned in Schedule No. 3, also annexed to the said plaint, as also to recover the money in cash mentioned in Schedule No. 5, and for confirmation of right in respect of the money advanced on loans, mentioned in Schedule No. 4, laid at Rupees 49,981, being the sum total of Rs. 1,465, which is three times the Sudder Jumma of the Mehals, mentioned in Schedule No. 1; Rs. 7,324, the selling price of the properties mentioned in Schedules No. 2 and No. 3 ; and Rs. 2,800, the amount of the properties mentioned in the Schedules No. 4 and No. 5.

That a written statement, by way of answer to the said plaint, was filed by the said —— on the —— day of ——, 186—.

That the said ——, the other respondent, did not file any answer in the said suit.

That evidence, both oral and documentary, was then adduced on behalf of the plaintiff, your petitioner, and also on behalf of the said defendant.

That the issues for trial were settled and recorded by a proceeding of the Court, dated ——, 186—.

That the hearing of the suit took place before the Judge of the Civil Court of ——, on the ——, 186—, into which Court it had been brought for decision by an order of the High Court, dated ——, 186—, when he was pleased to deliver his judgment and decree as follows :—That the plaintiff's case be dismissed with costs, and the costs of the defendant, meaning the said answering defendant, be realised from the plaintiffs, with interest at the rate of one rupee per cent. every month from this date.

That your petitioner, being dissatisfied with the said last-mentioned judgment and decree, appealed

therefrom to the High Court of Judicature at Fort
William, in Bengal, and on the —— day of ——,
18—, your petitioner filed her grounds of appeal.

That the hearing of the appeal took place on the
—— day of ——, 18—, before the judges of the
said High Court, when they were pleased to deliver
their judgment, and to order and decree as follows :
—"That the decision of the Lower Court be affirmed, and this appeal dismissed. And it is further
ordered and decreed that the plaintiff-appellant do
pay to the defendant-respondent who appeared in
this appeal the sum of ——, being the amount of
costs incurred by her in this Court, with interest
thereon, at the rate of 12 per cent. per annum, from
this date to date of realisation thereof."

That your petitioner, feeling aggrieved by the
last-mentioned judgment and decree, filed the ordinary petition in the High Court at Calcutta, praying
for leave to appeal against the said decree to your
Most Excellent Majesty in Council, which leave was
granted on the usual terms, which have since been
duly complied with.

Your petitioner therefore humbly prays that
your Most Excellent Majesty in Council
will be graciously pleased to take her
appeal into consideration, and to grant
her your Majesty's order of summons
upon the said respondents to appear and
put in their answer thereto, and that
service of the said order upon their
solicitors or agents may be deemed good
service, and that an early day may be

appointed for the hearing of the said
appeal by the Lords of the Judicial Committee of the Privy Council, and that the
said judgment and decree of the said
Civil Court of Zillah (———), dated ———,
and also the said judgment and decree of
the said High Court, bearing date the
——— day of ———, may be reversed,
altered, or varied; or that your petitioner
may have such further or other relief in
the premises as to your Majesty, in your
great wisdom, shall seem meet.

And your petitioner will ever pray, &c.

PETITION OF APPEAL.

IN THE PRIVY COUNCIL.

On appeal from the Court of Queen's Bench for
Lower Canada.

BETWEEN

Full title.

Appellant,

and

Respondent.

To

The Queen's Most Excellent Majesty in Council.

The humble petition of the above-named
appellant,

SHEWETH,

That on or about the ——— day of ———, 186—,
your petitioner filed his declaration in an action in

the Superior Court for Lower Canada, in the district of Montreal, against ——, respondent.

State shortly cause of action.

That the said respondent duly appeared and pleaded to the said declaration.

That the said cause having duly proceeded to issue, was tried by the said Court, and evidence relating to the matters in dispute between the said parties was entered into.

That on or about the —— day of ——, 186—, judgment was given by the said Court for your petitioner, condemning the said respondent to pay your petitioner the sum of ——, with interest on the said sum of ——, from the —— day of ——, 18—, until paid; also condemning the said respondent to pay the costs of suit.

That the said respondent appealed from the said judgment to the said Court of Queen's Bench for Lower Canada.

That on or about the —— day of —— 186—, the said Court of Queen's Bench for Lower Canada delivered judgment reversing and making void the said judgment of the said Supreme Court for Lower Canada, and rejecting your petitioner's action with costs, as well in the court of first instance as of the then appeal.

That your petitioner feeling himself aggrieved by the said judgment of the Court of Queen's Bench for Lower Canada, moved the said Court for leave to appeal to your Majesty in Council, and the said Court by their order allowed the said motion, and granted such leave upon conditions which have since been duly complied with by your petitioner.

That a printed transcript of the proceedings in the said cause, including the said last-mentioned motion and order, has been transmitted to your Majesty in Council.

Your petitioner, therefore, most humbly prays that your Majesty in Council will be pleased to take his said appeal into your most gracious consideration, and to grant him your Majesty's order of summons upon the said respondent to appear and put in his answer thereto, and that service of the said order of summons upon the agent of the said respondent may be deemed good service, and that an early day may be appointed for the hearing of the said appeal, and that the said judgment of the said Court of Queen's Bench for Lower Canada may be reversed, altered, or varied, and the said judgment of the said Supreme Court for Lower Canada affirmed in whole or in part, or that your petitioner may have such further and other relief in the premises as to your Majesty in your great wisdom shall seem meet.

And your petitioner will ever pray, &c.

PETITION FOR SPECIAL LEAVE TO APPEAL.

In the Privy Council.

And in the matter of an action lately depending in
the Supreme Court of ——.

Name of court.

Between

Plaintiff,   Full title.

and

Defendant.

To

The Queen's most excellent Majesty in Council.

The humble petition of ——

Here describe the petitioner.

Sheweth,

That on or about the —— day of ——, 186—,
one —— filed his declaration in an action upon
the case on the plea side of the Supreme Court
of ——, against your petitioner, to recover £300,

State here the cause of action.

That on or about the —— day of the said month
of ——, your petitioner duly appeared and pleaded
to the said declaration.

That, the said cause being at issue, it was tried
by the said Court on or about the —— day of ——
in the same year, and evidence both oral and
documentary, relating to the matters in dispute

between the said parties, was entered into; and after the plaintiff had closed his case, the judge entered a non-suit upon the ground that there was no evidence in support of the plaintiff's declaration, with leave reserved to the said plaintiff to move to set the said non-suit aside, and to enter a verdict for the said plaintiff for nominal damages with costs certified.

That on or about the —— day of ——, in the same year, the said plaintiff moved the said Court for a rule nisi to set aside the said non-suit, and to enter a verdict for the said plaintiff for nominal damages, as aforesaid, *or for a new trial in the said cause.*

That on or about the —— day of the said month of —— cause was shown by your petitioner against the said rule.

That on or about the —— day of the same month of —— the said Court gave judgment, and ordered that the said rule to set aside the said non-suit and to enter a verdict for the said plaintiff for nominal damages,—that is to say, forty shillings,—be made absolute, and costs certified upon the ground

Here state shortly the ground upon which the Court gave judgment.

That your petitioner thereupon applied for a new trial, which the said Court refused to grant.

That your petitioner feels aggrieved by the said judgment of the said Court, ordering that the said non-suit be set aside, and a verdict to be entered for the said plaintiff, with costs, and by the refusal to your petitioner of a new trial, for that your petitioner

Here state reasons why petitioner feels aggrieved.

That your petitioner

Here state the grounds upon which the applicant conceives himself entitled to have special leave to appeal, notwithstanding the amount in dispute being under the appealable amount.

That your petitioner is able, ready, and willing to enter into the required securities for the costs of an appeal herein.

Your petitioner, therefore, most humbly prays that your Most Excellent Majesty in Council will be graciously pleased to order that your petitioner shall have special leave to appeal from the said judgment of the said Supreme Court of , and that the said Supreme Court may be ordered to transmit forthwith the transcript of the pleadings and evidence and other proceedings in

II

the said matter to the Privy Council
office, and that the said judgment of the
said Court, ordering that the non-suit
entered on the trial of the said cause be
set aside, and a verdict be entered for the
said plaintiff for forty shillings damages
and costs certified, be reversed, and that
your Majesty may be graciously pleased
to make such further or other order as to
your Majesty in Council may appear just
and proper.

And your petitioner will ever pray, &c.

AT THE COURT AT BUCKINGHAM PALACE,

the 13th day of June, 1853.

PRESENT :

THE QUEEN'S MOST EXCELLENT MAJESTY.

HIS ROYAL HIGHNESS PRINCE ALBERT.

LORD PRESIDENT.	EARL OF ABERDEEN.
LORD STEWARD.	EARL OF CLARENDON.
DUKE OF NEWCASTLE.	VISCOUNT PALMERSTON.
DUKE OF WELLINGTON.	MR. HERBERT.
LORD CHAMBERLAIN.	SIR JAMES GRAHAM, BT.

WHEREAS there was this day read at the Board a report from the Right Honourable the Lords of the Judicial Committee of the Privy Council, dated the 30th May last past, humbly setting forth that the Lords of the Judicial Committee have taken into consideration the practice of the Committee with a view to greater economy, despatch, and efficiency in the appellate jurisdiction of Her Majesty in Council, and that their Lordships have agreed humbly to report to Her Majesty that it is expedient that certain changes should be made in the existing practice in appeals, and recommending that certain rules and regulations therein set forth should henceforth be observed, obeyed, and carried into execution, provided Her Majesty is pleased to approve the same :

Her Majesty, having taken the said report into consideration, was pleased, by and with the advice of her Privy Council, to approve thereof, and of the rules and regulations set forth therein, in the words following, videlicet :—

Appellant, when successful, may recover costs of appeal.

I. That, any former usage or practice of Her Majesty's Privy Council notwithstanding, an appellant who shall succeed in obtaining a reversal or material alteration of any judgment, decree, or order appealed from, shall be entitled to recover the costs of the appeal from the respondent, except in cases in which the Lords of the Judicial Committee may think fit otherwise to direct.

Transcripts to be sent to Registrar of Privy Council.

II. That the Registrar or other proper officer having the custody of records in any Court or special jurisdiction from which an appeal is brought to Her Majesty in Council be directed to send by post, with all possible despatch, one certified copy of the transcript record in each cause to the Registrar of Her Majesty's Privy Council, Whitehall ; and that all such transcripts be registered in the Privy Council Office, with the date of their

arrival, the **names of the parties, and the
date** of the **sentence** appealed from; **and**
that such **transcript be** accompanied **by a
correct and** complete index of all the papers,
documents, and exhibits in the cause; **and**
that the Registrar of the Court appealed
from, **or** other proper officer of such Court,
be directed to omit from such transcript all
merely formal documents, provided such
omission be stated and certified in the said
index of papers; and that especial care be
taken not to allow any document to **be set**
forth more than once **in such** transcript;
and that no other certified copies of **the**
record be transmitted **to** agents in England
by or on behalf **of the parties** in the suit;
and that the fees and expenses incurred and
paid **for the preparation of** such transcript
be stated and certified upon it by the
Registrar **or** other officer preparing the same.

III. That when the record of proceedings Transcripts
may be
printed
abroad.
or evidence in the cause appealed has been
printed or partly printed abroad, the Regis-
trar or other proper officer of the Court
from which the appeal is brought shall be
bound to send home the same in a printed
form, either wholly or so far as the same
may have **been** printed, and that he do

certify the same to be correct, on two copies, by signing his name on every printed sheet, and by affixing the seal, if any, of the Court appealed from to these copies, with the sanction of the Court.

And that in all cases in which the parties in appeals shall think fit to have the proceedings printed abroad, they shall be at liberty to do so, provided they cause fifty copies of the same to be printed in folio, and transmitted, at their expense, to the Registrar of the Privy Council, two of which printed copies shall be certified as above by the officers of the Court appealed from ; and in this case no further expense for copying or printing the record will be incurred or allowed in England.

Written transcripts to be printed by her Majesty's Printer.

IV. That on the arrival of a written transcript of appeal at the Privy Council Office, Whitehall, the appellant or the agent of the appellant prosecuting the same shall be at liberty to call on the Registrar of the Privy Council to cause it, or such part thereof as may be necessary for the hearing of the case, and likewise all such parts thereof as the respondent or his agent may require, to be printed by Her Majesty's Printer, or by any other printer on the same

terms, the appellant or his agent engaging
to pay the cost of preparing a copy for the
printer at a rate not exceeding one shilling
per brief sheet, and likewise the cost of
printing such record or appendix, and that
one hundred copies of the same be struck
off, whereof thirty copies are to be delivered
to the agents on each side, and forty kept
for the use of the Judicial Committee ; and
that no other fees for solicitors' copies of the
transcript, or for drawing the joint appendix,
be henceforth allowed, the solicitors on both
sides being allowed to have access to the
original papers at the Council Office, and to
extract or cause to be extracted and copied
such parts thereof as are necessary for the
preparation of the petition of appeal, at the
stationer's charge not exceeding one shilling
per brief sheet.

V. That a certain time be fixed within
which it shall be the duty of the appellant
or his agent to make such application for
the printing of the transcript, and that such
time be within the space of six calendar
months from the arrival of the transcript
and the registration thereof in all matters
brought by appeal from her Majesty's colonies and plantations east of the Cape of

Transcripts
to be printed
within a
certain
time.

Good Hope, or from the territories of the
East India Company, and within the space
of three months in all matters brought by
appeal from any other part of her Majesty's
dominions abroad; and that in default of
the appellant or his agent taking effectual
steps for the prosecution of the appeal within
such time or times respectively, the appeal
shall stand dismissed without further order,
and that a report of the same be made to
the Judicial Committee by the Registrar of
the Privy Council at their Lordships' next
sitting.

Appeals
may be
heard in the
form of a
special case.

VI. That whenever it shall be found that
the decision of a matter on appeal is likely
to turn exclusively on a question of law, the
agents of the parties, with the sanction of
the Registrar of the Privy Council, may sub-
mit such question of law to the Lords of the
Judicial Committee in the form of a special
case, and print such parts only of the transcript as may be necessary for the discussion
of the same; provided that nothing herein
contained shall in any way bar or prevent
the Lords of the Judicial Committee from
ordering the full discussion of the whole
case, if they shall so think fit; and that in
order to promote such arrangements and

simplification of the matter in dispute, the Registrar of the Privy Council may call the agents of the parties before him, and having heard them, and examined the transcript, may report to the Committee as to the nature of the proceedings.

And Her Majesty is further pleased to order, and it is hereby ordered, that the foregoing rules and regulations be punctually observed, obeyed, and carried into execution in all appeals or petitions and complaints in the nature of appeals brought to Her Majesty, or to her heirs and successors, in Council, from Her Majesty's colonies and plantations abroad, and from the Channel Islands or the Isle of Man, and from the territories of the East India Company, whether the same be from courts of justice or from special jurisdictions, other than appeals from Her Majesty's Courts of Vice-Admiralty, to which the said rules are not to be applied.

Whereof the judges and officers of Her Majesty's courts of justice abroad, and the judges and officers of the Superior Courts of the East India Company, and all other persons whom it may concern, are to take notice, and govern themselves accordingly.

W. L. BATHURST.

AT THE COURT AT BUCKINGHAM PALACE,

the 31*st day of March,* 1855.

PRESENT :

THE QUEEN'S MOST EXCELLENT MAJESTY IN
COUNCIL.

WHEREAS doubts have arisen with reference to the power of the Judicial Committee of the Privy Council to suspend or relax, under certain special circumstances, the regulations in appeal causes established by Her Majesty's Order in Council of the 13th June, 1853 : Her Majesty, by and with the advice of her Privy Council, is pleased to order, and it is hereby ordered, that in appeal cases in which a petition of appeal to Her Majesty shall have been lodged, and referred by Her Majesty to the Judicial Committee, the said regulations shall be subject to any order or direction which, in the opinion of the Lords of the Judicial Committee, the justice of any particular case may seem to require.

C. C. GREVILLE.

INDEX.

I

THE END.

BRADBURY, EVANS, AND CO., PRINTERS, WHITEFRIARS.

Webster on Conditions of Sale.—The Law relating to Particulars and Conditions of Sale on a Sale of Land. By WILLIAM FREDERICK WEBSTER, Esq., Barrister-at-Law. Royal 8vo. 1889. Price 1l. 1s. cloth.

Wheaton's Elements of International Law.—Third English Edition, with Notes. By A. C. BOYD, Esq., Barrister-at-Law. Royal 8vo. 1889. Price 1l. 10s. cloth.

"Wheaton stands too high for criticism, whilst Mr. Boyd's merits as an editor are almost as well established."—*Law Times*.

Stringer's Oaths and Affirmations in Great Britain and Ireland; being a Collection of Statutes, Cases, and Forms, with Notes and Practical Directions for the use of Commissioners for Oaths, and of all Courts of Civil Procedure and Offices attached thereto. [In succession to "Braithwaite's Oaths."] By FRANCIS A. STRINGER, of the Central Office, Supreme Court of Judicature, one of the Editors of the "Annual Practice." Crown 8vo. 1890. Price 3s. 6d. cloth.

"Indispensable to all Commissioners."—*Solicitors' Journal*.

Geare's Investment of Trust Funds.—Incorporating the Trustee Act, 1888. Second Edition. Including the Trusts Investment Act, 1889. By EDWARD ARUNDEL GEARE, Esq., Barrister-at-Law. Royal 12mo. 1889. Price 7s. 6d. cloth.

Browne and Theobald's Law of Railway Companies.—Being a Collection of the Acts and Orders relating to Railway Companies in England and Ireland, with Notes of all the Cases decided thereon, and Appendix of Bye-Laws and Standing Orders of the House of Commons. Second Edition. By J. H. BALFOUR BROWNE, Esq., one of Her Majesty's Counsel, and H. S. THEOBALD, Esq., Barrister-at-Law. Royal 8vo. 1888. Price 1l. 15s. cloth.

"Contains in a very concise form the whole law of railways."—*Times*.

Macnamara's Law of Carriers.—A Digest of the Law of Carriers of Goods and Passengers by Land and Internal Navigation. By WALTER HENRY MACNAMARA, Esq., Barrister-at-Law, Registrar to the Railway Commission. Royal 8vo. 1888. Price 1l. 8s. cloth.

Shirley's Sketch of the Criminal Law.—Second Edition. By CHARLES STEPHEN HUNTER, Esq., Barrister-at-Law. Demy 8vo. 1889. Price 7s. 6d. cloth.

Shirley's Selection of Leading Cases in the Criminal Law, with Notes. By WALTER S. SHIRLEY, Esq., Barrister-at-Law. Demy 8vo. 1888. Price 6s. cloth.

Shirley's Leading Cases in the Common Law, with Notes.—Third Edition. By WALTER S. SHIRLEY, Esq., Barrister-at-Law. Demy 8vo. 1886. Price 16s. cloth.

Wharton's Law Lexicon.—Forming an Epitome of the Law of England, and containing full explanations of the Technical Terms and Phrases thereof, both ancient and modern; including the various Legal Terms used in Commercial Business, together with a Translation of the Latin Maxims, and selected Titles from the Civil, Scotch and Indian Law. Eighth Edition. By J. M. LELY, Esq., Barrister-at-Law. Super-royal 8vo. 1889. Price 1l. 18s. cloth.

Harris' Hints on Advocacy.—Conduct of Cases Civil and Criminal. Classes of Witnesses and Suggestions for Cross-examining them, &c., &c. By RICHARD HARRIS, one of Her Majesty's Counsel. Ninth Edition. With a new Chapter on "Tactics." Royal 12mo. 1889. Price 7s. 6d. cloth.

"Full of good sense and just observation. A very complete Manual of the Advocates' art in Trial by Jury."—*Solicitors' Journal*.

www.ingramcontent.com/pod-product-compliance
Lightning Source LLC
Chambersburg PA
CBHW020538270326
41927CB00006B/635